# Bootlicked
# to Balanced

# Bootlicked to Balanced

## Healing the Mind, Freeing the Spirit

Candi Dugas

**To order additional copies of this book, contact:**
Xlibris Corporation
1-888-795-4274
www.Xlibris.com
Orders@Xlibris.com
58041

# table of contents

# *dedication*

*My Lord God, I have no idea where I am going. I do not know for certain where it will end. Nor do I really know myself, and the fact that I think that I am following your will does not mean that I am actually doing so. But I believe that the desire to please you does in fact please you. And I hope I have that desire in all that I am doing. I hope that I will never do anything apart from that desire. And I know that if I do this you will lead me by the right road though I may know nothing about it. Therefore will I trust you always though I may seem to be lost and in the shadow of death. I will not fear, for you are ever with me, and you will never leave me to face my perils alone.*

*Thomas Merton*
*Thoughts in Solitude*[1]

**to God . . . thank you**
**—candi**

# *acknowledgements*

thank you for all you did, and of course, for all of your prayers:

my family and friends
especially mom, jordan, kimberlee

all of my teachers—inside and outside of the academy

all of my bible study students, the first readers of this work

# *author's note*

*boot-licked (adj.)—to be accepting of, without question and/or push-back, the philosophies and teachings of authority*

My marketing firm asked me a question that I expected, but dreaded because it is one that I do not like to answer. "For whom did you write this book?" I dreaded answering because I knew my marketing folks would not like my answer—everyone. I know we cannot market to everyone. Yet I did write this book for them—maybe I should say—anyone.

This book *is* for anyone—anyone who is seeking something more or something else than what they have known before now. It is for anyone who is seeking truths that are truer for themselves. It is for anyone who desires to be healed and whole.

> "'Thou art made for wholeness,
> Body, mind, spirit: one creative synthesis,
> Moving in perfect harmony within, without,
> With fellow man and nature all around
> To make Heaven where Hell is found.'"[2]

I am not suggesting that I have all of the answers or all of the information. Far from it. In fact, in many ways, I often feel I am only beginning my journey. The more answers I receive or discover, the more questions that form within me. Through this work, simply, I am sharing some information, some Christian Scripture, and some forms of a discipline that I have found to be helpful for me in seeking and finding the more and the else.

My hope is that you will take what is contained within and find some piece or pieces of it that resonate within you. Then lead others to this book.

Share with them your response(s) to it. Let us converse and debate and love together. Let us fully enjoy and embrace this beautiful gift of life that God has bestowed upon us.

best,
candi dugas

# *forethought*

This is who I was meant to be
Full and free
But my fullness
Makes others nervous
And my dad—
Isn't . . . wasn't around to protect me

Only he could do it
Like it needed to be done
I'm more like him than anybody else
Would've been great for him to help me be . . .
But he wasn't—
Here . . . there for me
Well, at least not in the ways I thought he should

If he had been, maybe they wouldn't have sucked
So much of me out of me before
I was strong enough to stop it
Couldn't . . . can't help but get angry sometimes about it
Couldn't . . . can't help but declare that it went on
For far too long
Such unnecessary struggle—or was it
Necessary
Couldn't it have all been avoided
If he had been . . .

# *one*

## **still**

*Introducing Meditation*

> *I remember sitting at one of the most beautiful, oasis-like areas on the campus of the University of Florida sometime midway through my college years—wondering who the hell I was. Time and time again, I returned to those oases throughout campus, seeking answers and only finding more questions. I was a long way from the confident and creative above-average student I had always known myself to be. I had no sense of where I was headed or how to get there. I felt as if my life was falling apart, and somewhere inside, I felt wholly responsible for myself for the first time. Furthermore, I did not know where God was . . .*

I was seeking healing and wholeness, though I would not have used those words at the time. I did not consider myself sick or afflicted with dis-ease. I did not consider myself broken. Had someone presented those terms to me, I would have wholly rejected them. I would have found them to be a little too deep and involved . . . and negative. Nothing was *that* wrong with me. Yeah, right, I was just moping around campus, missing classes and spending my evenings among the underbrush next to pond water.

It would be some years more before I discovered an expanded understanding of meditation as a Christian spiritual discipline. Meditation was key for me in finding God again, in finding myself—though not necessarily in that order. Meditation led me toward becoming healed and whole—a state of being that I continue to pursue today.

Too often we only associate the need for healing with our bodies, ignoring that we also have a spirit and a soul *(more about this in the next chapter)*. Any or all of these three parts of ourselves can be injured and require healing. We will generally tend to our physical wounds, leaving those of the spirit and soul to linger, become "infected," and wreak all kinds of havoc on our entire being. Finally, when these more obscure wounds finally affect our bodies, we begin to seek the source of our problem(s).

However, only when physical treatments are unsuccessful might we pursue deeper understanding within our spirits and souls, despite the fact that "90 percent of all physical problems have psychological roots."[3] Most of us live our lives—enduring challenges, disappointments and pains—without understanding the impact on our beings from neglecting our feelings. "Those feelings are NOT dead unless they are resolved . . . those feelings from long ago have been and are still being registered at and in the cellular level of our Being."[4]

Once I began heightening my awareness of my inner being, I was a healthier person. I wholly supported and encouraged activities that connected people this way—counseling, meditation, etc. However, recently, I became acutely conscious of how critical this awareness really is to be at our best—for ourselves and for those whom we love.

Recently, I discovered that I had a phobia. A phobia??? Again, like in college, I would have denied this assessment had someone presented it to me before I experienced an episode. I would have readily admitted scars and issues, but a phobia? Nope, that's for really imbalanced people. I am a meditative, counseling-seeking, self-aware woman of God. One thing I am *not* is phobic. I would have argued anyone down on this point—until the day that I almost hyperventilated in my car. I was on the phone with one of my dear friends barely able to articulate my feelings. I feared, deeply, that I would be seriously hurt emotionally by a potential love interest because of a conversation. This conversation was completely unrelated to our budding personal relationship.

> "There is a condition that extends beyond the usual and normal stresses in life that is closely related to [daily] STRESSORS . . . This condition often manifests in a person when unidentified and unresolved feelings—deep STRESSORS—are present in the body. This condition is known as a 'Phobia.' Whatever the feeling/belief may be that has created the phobia, it is usually rooted in some kind of FEAR. This fear has been stored, for who knows how long in the subconscious mind which is connected to the nervous system. When this fear is triggered quickly by a sight, a smell, a touch, or a sound, it arouses feelings of anxiety, fright, and panic—almost like someone has a gun to your head—and the nervous system jumps into action, responding to the trigger by supplying all the unpleasant reactions

that have been created by the fear stored in the sub-conscious, and a wild imagination."[5]

As a writer, I certainly have a vivid imagination! Seriously, though, even as I write this book, I am healing from some "deep STRESSORS" that first occurred in my life 30+ years ago. From them I developed abandonment issues. Fear of abandonment is one of the most common fears we have as human beings. Other common fears are of being alone, criticism, falling, illness, going crazy, rejection, and speaking in public.[6] I first felt abandoned as a little girl when my father's visits often turned out differently than I understood they would be. I visited with my father about three times a year. For the time in between visits I counted the months, weeks, and days until the next one—looking forward to *my* time with *my* daddy—just me and Daddy. Usually, it was not just me and Daddy. I had to share him with his latest love interest. He never communicated this requirement to share him until we were in the car on the way to "her place." In that moment, I felt abandoned. And it happened over and over again. And, I never said anything about it.

In later years, as I began to date boys and men, no matter how I tried to make wise choices and ask questions, I generally ended up in the same situation. Abandoned by the ones I desired to be in my life. I did not know I had unhealed wounds. I did not know that I was adopting erroneous beliefs about myself and my situation. I was not aware of how these misperceptions were manifesting into life conditions I did not want and thought I was combating. "Whatever our belief systems are, we draw situations to us in our lives like a magnet draws iron filings, that naturally validate our beliefs, regardless of what they are."[7] Consequently again and again, the same kind of man was drawn to me and I to him, a man who would not show up for me, because I had not healed.

So there I was in my car acting as if "someone [had] a gun to [my] head," from a totally, and I mean totally, unrelated conversation. I cannot explain at this point why that was the day, why that was the time. Maybe I will never know, and I am not sure that this knowledge is even relevant. I totally trust God's sense of timing. The days since my panic attack have been intense; I am not sure that I was strong and deep and broad enough in my younger years to handle this kind of pain. As I wrote earlier, I am not completely healed yet as I complete this book. I am still working with myself and my counselor toward that end. I am confident, though, that the healing moment will come, and it will be complete at that time.

This experience and others I have had compel me to share my knowledge and to implore all with whom I come in contact to tend to our *whole* selves. We lose way too much as individuals, as families, as communities, as a world when we do not. Often we are not aware of what we have lost until, sometimes, it is too late to remedy our actions—or inaction.

---

Welcome to this meditation journey.

This experience together is designed for early morning meditation over a four-week period. Meditating in the morning yields sweet benefits. Among the benefits is the framing of our day. Meditation allows us to center our spirits as well as cause us to be still and to be better in-touch with our true selves. Above all else, this experience ought not to cause any stress or strain. So, if you determine that morning simply will not work for you, select your best time and be still.

However, if you do choose the morning and you are not a morning person, practice waking up earlier than you are accustomed **before** you start your meditations. This will help you keep separate your ability to wake up early from your ability to meditate. We want our times of meditation to be beneficial and enjoyable. Feeling frustrated about an early rising defeats this desire. Practice by setting a time at least five minutes earlier than you rise currently. Then increase your time until you can rise 15-30 minutes earlier than you need in order to prepare for your day. This ought to be enough time to read your lesson and meditate.

If after practicing you find an early rise continuing to elude you, all is not lost. Instead of planning to read and meditate in the morning, you may read the lesson in the evening, prior to going to bed. Then meditate in the morning after briefly reviewing the lesson. The lesson and meditation can still frame your day.

During the time of meditation, ideally, you do not want to end until you have sensed an understanding with which to go forward. *(This will be explained later.)* Therefore, you want to get up in enough time so that your moments in mediation are relaxed and not hurried. *(If 30 minutes is not enough time, feel free to extend your meditative time.)* So that you do not run late preparing for your day, you may want to set a gentle alarm to signal the end of your meditation. We want to keep this experience calm and loose.

*Establishing the Foundation*
Let's clarify two definitions:

### Meditation
Generally, to meditate means, "to muse over, to contemplate or ponder; to intend or plan."[8]

Books on meditation are a little more specific. Consider the following definitions:

Meditation is . . .

". . . a training method to control thought processes. It is a time which we can build, create, by directing thought."[9]

". . . the process by which we go about deepening our attention and awareness, refining them, and putting them to greater practical use in our lives."[10]

### Christian-based Meditation
*A time of choosing to think deeply on Scripture and other inspired writings rooted in the Christian tradition, stimulating the mind and stirring the spirit—seeking peace for one's life.*

Our plan for this book is to begin slowly, patiently increasing our time in meditation. Remember this is a process and there is no pressure to do it right or to do it a certain way. We have set a couple of definitions for the purpose of this journey. Let us now delve a little more into what meditation is and what it is not.

Meditation is more of a preparation for prayer than it is prayer itself. It is an exercise for the human mind so that you will know how to pray. It is a time of connecting with self and with God. You may receive wisdom and guidance from God, or you may just become calm long enough to think clearly. Meditation is more of a time to receive and be, rather than quiet moments to create a "to do" list. We can gain deeper understanding of who we think we are, who God created us to be, and any differences between those realities. It is a time to reconcile the truths of our lives with the lives we can have. It is a time to connect with an inner power that we sometimes forget exists.

While meditation is a time of preparation, we have to be ready to meditate—prepare to prepare. Entering meditation means being/becoming ready to confront some issues and/or feelings of which we may have been unaware. It means we will hear our inner voices express thoughts and/or emotions that have been hidden or, indeed, buried. The trick is to allow the revelations and to hear our inner voices without trying to make it better, *immediately*. Remember, meditation is simple. It's just not all that easy; it is hard work simply to be present in the meditative moment.[11]

In meditation all we want to do is to pay attention to the moment at hand in a particular way without drawing any particular conclusion. If a question comes to mind, do not try to answer it or seek God's answer to it. For the moment, simply have a question. Be sure to journal it, because the answer will come. When focusing attention on the meditative moment without the weight of conclusions, we cultivate the ability to experience more of life's moments on a daily basis. "If we are not fully present for many of those moments, we may not only miss what is most valuable in our lives, but also fail to realize the richness and the depth of our possibilities for growth and transformation."[12]

> "What we steadily, consciously, habitually think we are, that we tend to become."[13]

Remember that our definition of meditation is "a time to think deeply . . ." We will come to experience, as we purposely set aside time to meditate, that our time of meditation will extend beyond that specific time apart to be still. Then transformation—or reclamation—takes place.

Some Christians reading this book may have already determined that they are not particularly familiar with meditation as a spiritual discipline. Yet it is one that is available to us. Surveying the bookstores one would not find many books labeled as meditation books for Christians. Generally these books are called "devotionals." We Christians have left the discipline of meditation to those of other religions—Buddhism, New Age, etc. Yet the Bible clearly encourages us to meditate.

> "I have hidden Your word in my heart, that I may not sin against You." *(Psalm 119:11)*

> "Do not let this Book of the Law depart from your mouth; meditate on it day and night . . ." *(Joshua 1:8)*

This book attempts to define meditation as an important discipline for Christians that can help our lives become powerful testaments to the grace and freedom available as a disciple of Jesus Christ. Meditation is important because it affects the **mind**. It is "a time of choosing to think deeply . . ." What do you think about most of the time? *How* do you think most of the time? Half-full or half-empty? **The mind is the most powerful part of who we are. What our mind knows, chooses, decides, and thinks affects everything else about us.**

*Purpose and an Eternal Perspective*

> *"'I went to the woods because I wished to live deliberately, to front only the essential facts of life, and see if I could not learn what it had to teach, and not, when I came to die, discover that I had not lived.'"[14]*

I am always seeking the purpose in something or else I find that I have little desire to do it or be a part of it. "What has this got to do with the big picture?" "Where's the meaning?" While these questions sometimes make me a little "heady," there is even purpose in doing nothing. It's called rest and not taking life too seriously. *(smile)*

Being still helps us discover, understand, and participate in purpose.

Every life on this earth has purpose. There is a reason that each and every one of us was born. God wastes nothing, not the smallest atom, so certainly not a human being, a whole conglomeration of atoms!

In his book, *The Leadership Secrets of Jesus*, Mike Murdock asserts that our [purpose]

> "will always *solve a problem*. Your life is a solution to someone in trouble. Find those who need you and what you have to offer. Build your life around that contribution."[15]

So then, discovering the problem we came to solve will lead us to our purpose. And I know without a doubt that the solution is an important one. God does not create, does not call anything into being if it need not be.

> "As the rain and the snow come down from heaven, and do not return to it without watering the earth and making it bud and flourish, so that it yields seed for the sower and bread for the eater, so is my word that goes out from my mouth: It will not return to me empty, but will accomplish what I desire and achieve the purpose for which I sent it." *(Isaiah 55:10, 11)*

Whether we deem our purpose to be local or global, we all have a purpose that affects the entire world. Such a notion can be daunting so when we sense ourselves shrinking back from this reality, we can limit our consideration of this notion to just what we see immediately before us. Like eating an elephant one bite at a time, we can put on temporary blinders, and just handle our immediate surroundings. Little by little we can sneak peeks from behind the blinders, broadening our scope. We can take small steps beyond our comfort zones, realizing we are stronger than we thought. As we continue to meditate, we continue to grow in understanding of who we are and increasing in faith and courage. Eventually we take a deep breath, discard the blinders, and take a huge leap forward into our place—our very unique place in the world that isn't so huge after all!

We have pondered the importance of meditation as a practiced discipline in one's life. We considered how choosing to "think deeply on Scripture" directs our thoughts and understanding, leading to a powerfully peaceful life. This kind of life is a testament to the total freedom through grace available to those of us who are contemporary disciples of Jesus. We have discussed purpose. Let us also contemplate our eternal perspectives.

Some people term this notion "considering the big picture." Others label it "putting first things first." And then there is the expression, "keeping the main thing, the main thing." Essentially all expressions purport an eternal perspective. This concept means that we give attention, energy, and work *only* to what is truly important. This concept means that when we perceive situations, circumstances, and issues—we perceive them more accurately by only using eternal *(as opposed to temporal)* and spiritual *(as opposed to physical)* principles to direct our thoughts and subsequent actions.

Absolutely meditation has been the discipline that opened the door to eternal perspective for me. All kinds of activity can occur around—even within me—and they can carry with them certain physical realities that may lead to less than desirable outcomes. However, with the underlying eternal truth to balance my understanding of the activity, I am more at peace. Remember, this kind of peace exists even when the outcomes of my situation are less than desirable.

When we live in this manner, we more completely fulfill our purposes, following our better paths, running our preferred races, and more is right with us and our lives. *(Again, keep in mind that all things being right and peaceful does not necessarily mean that there are no challenges, conflict, or pain. Obstacles still exist. We simply know how to maneuver among them. Louisa May Alcott wrote, "I'm not afraid of storms, for I'm learning how to sail my ship.")*

Ecclesiastes is an excellent book of the Bible to study as we consider the eternal perspective. In this book, the author, the "Teacher," whom most scholars strongly believe is Solomon—is at the end of his days on earth and is struggling with the meaning of life. Throughout most of the book, he concludes that "everything is meaningless."[16] The Teacher examines various aspects of life from almost every imaginable angle and still winds up at the same place—it's all meaningless, "a chasing after the wind."[17] Every time I read this book, I find the Teacher's cynicism rather humorous. I almost see him as a stand-up comic, using the stage as a platform upon which to comment on the issues of life.

One of the most well-known, oft-used passages from this book is from chapter three, verses one through eight, "There is a time for everything and a season for every activity under heaven . . ." Most of the time, we encounter this passage when someone passes from this life to the next. When someone's body dies, we have many questions:

- Why?
- Why her?
- Why now?

- Why in this way?
- Why?

And the eventual answer is—it was time. And who controls time? God. So why even ask why? God is sovereign and God does what God needs to do when God needs to do it. Therefore, we turn to Ecclesiastes 3:1-8 to comfort us by settling our spirits to a point of not asking why. It simply was time.

With that being so, why do we continue to ask why—or any other question for that matter—for which we seek God for the answers? Why do we ask . . .

- . . . if we will marry?
- . . . who will we marry?
- . . . when will we marry?
- . . . will I have children?
- . . . will I have 2 girls and 2 boys as I desire?
- . . . will they be pretty/handsome?
- . . . will they be healthy?
- . . . will they be smart?
- . . . will they look like me/my spouse?
- . . . what day care/primary school should I send them to?
- . . . will I have enough money to send them to a good college?
- . . . will I become famous and realize my dream(s)?
- . . . will I accumulate wealth?
- . . . will my name be remembered long after my death?
- . . . will I have to put my parents in a nursing home?
- . . . will *I* have to go to a nursing home when I am old?

The list is infinite.

*Inside and Free*

We have all heard the descriptions of folks living their lives with masks on their faces. I would add, with armor on their entire bodies. Of course the point is that people with this description are living their daily lives masquerading as happy and whole—no worries. For my life, I determined some time ago that I wanted to live a truly happy and whole life—no masks and no armor. When people encounter me and sense I am happy and whole, well, that will be an authentic sense. Even in my challenging times, I hope to emanate a sense of joy and peace.

To live such a life, not only does it help, immensely, to perceive things as God perceives them, an eternal perspective. To live such a life, we have to walk in the reality of who we are and what is occurring in our lives. This kind of life means that we are living from the inside out.

Truly, it can be quite a challenge to live each day fully integrated with all of who we are. Yet we are not our authentic selves when we deny our issues, questions, and concerns. As our authentic selves, we are stronger and more connected to our families, friends, and communities. Life then is more vibrant and available to us. Meditation allows us the ability to be full participants in our lives. Meditation allows us to take the time to be still and intimate with God and ourselves. Prayerfully:

- we encounter issues or different perspectives of issues of which we were unaware.
- we receive revelation knowledge from God and from within ourselves.
- we experience some healing in our bodies and/or souls.
- we solidly maintain our peaceful assurance wherever we go.

What an excellent way to be in each day!

Yeah, that way of being sounds like freedom to me!

I venture that we all desire full freedom, but few of us are really prepared to pay the price for it, or to operate at a level of responsibility, to maintain it with integrity. Regrettably, my experience of Christianity has been short on freedom. Rather, my experience has leaned more toward tight control on our lives, lest we "backslide" into leading pervasively sinful lives.

Obviously, one who earnestly endeavors to reflect God, to profess a belief in Christ, and to allow the Holy Spirit to be an active entity in her/his life will not lead a pervasively sinful life. So, why cannot Christianity lead the way in proclaiming the freedom available to human beings, when Jesus Christ is our Lord and Savior? Here and there have been movements to rid Christians of a reputation of being meek and humble, unable to say no. Here and there have been movements to rid Christians of having to be lowly and poor. Yet, I still desire a movement that allows Christians to be, simply, fully free, embracing and enjoying life, re-presenting God in a way that draws the world rather than repel it.

My hope is that as you embark on this meditative journey with me, you will discover an ability to be still, cultivate an eternal perspective, be courageous enough to live from the inside out, and endeavor to live fully free.

Instructions

Consider the following general guide to meditating and refer to it as you meditate:

1) Find/create/use a quiet, calm, peaceful place.
2) Sit straight, yet comfortably, but not so much so that you will fall asleep. Do not cross arms or legs. Sitting straight without crossing limbs enhances blood and energy flow.[18]
3) Relax your hands, jaw, neck—any place you hold tension and stress.
4) Read the passage three times.
5) Close your eyes and reflect on it. Focus on a portion that can repeat in your mind.
6) If your mind begins to stray, decide to return to your focused passage.
7) Listen for your inner voice. Listen for God.
8) Be especially aware of any physical manifestations of God's presence experienced by your body (i. e., warmth, breezes, shaking hands, etc.)
9) Write down your experience.
10) Linger in the ending moments.

Important Notes:

1) Read and meditate daily to maximize benefits.
2) DO NOT READ AHEAD. This is a daily experience. Take each day as it comes and let each day be what it is.
3) When reading references come from the Christian Holy Bible, they are from the New International Version, unless otherwise noted.
4) If you miss a day, pick back up where you left off. Notice that the days are not dated, only numbered.

# *two*

## *breathe*

*My maternal grandmother was my first spiritual teacher. She taught me the traditional bedside prayers and ensured I said them each night before going to bed. The nuns at my elementary school were my next highly influential spiritual teachers, particularly Sister Christine in fifth grade. During that year's study of the rosary, I had my first powerfully quiet encounter with the Holy Spirit. For the entire week of intentionally praying the rosary before bed—whether I fell asleep in the middle of it or not—I experienced a peace and a power within myself like no other time in my life. As a typical 10 year-old, I suppose, I did not pursue it after the week was over. Then, while visiting my maternal great-aunt the summer I turned 13, the Holy Spirit washed over me at the closing ceremony of Vacation Bible School. Through sheets of tears, I confessed Christ as my Lord and Savior. Though it would be another few years before I was baptized and despite my inactivity with a church body, I felt solid in my faith and I knew where God was.*

*Somehow in college, though, I lost my sense of how to find God, and all that was solid became incredibly shaky. Somehow my traditional bedside prayers had become proverbial and lacked power. Replaying the same gospel music cassette on Sunday mornings after hours of partying Saturday night somehow lost its energy. I felt disconnected from almost everything. I did not even have my intellectual confidence as my grades were suffering, and I had no idea what my major should be. Not one course of study ignited passion within me. I could not point to anything that ignited passion within me—not even the Greek parties I had once lived for each weekend. Where was God . . .*

*week one*

## DAY ONE—*First Step*

I suspect you are reading this book because you seek a more peaceful and powerful way of living. Meditation—one way to such a lifestyle—may be new to you as a practiced discipline. Or, you may be seeking to reclaim its place in your life. In either case, though you desire it, practicing meditation may not be so easy—at first. Meditation is a simple discipline, yet it is not easy, especially in this society of hectic schedules and congested calendars. Consider an excerpt from the following meditation:

> Thursday Therapy
>
> Relax and Rest!
>
> Hebrews 4:9, 10
>
> *"Therefore, a time of rest and worship exists for God's people. Those who entered His place of rest also rested from their work as God did from His." (GOD'S WORD Version)*
>
> Everything is at such a fast pace these days. We run here and there to do this and that. Everything is urgent, top-priority. People can call us at any time on our cell phones. They usually call right in the middle of some important meeting or even during worship service—constantly reminding us that we need to do something else or talk to someone else. We often don't get the chance to enjoy the moment we're in. We might be at home while our brain is at work busy figuring out what needs to be done the next day. No wonder people are so anxious. There's a pill to help you calm down, wake-up and go to sleep because people are struggling to do things that should be natural. We have forgotten how to relax and rest.
>
> . . .
>
> Remember, the things that seem to matter do not matter. And the things that seem unimportant are really eternal. We should choose to spend most of our time doing things that will last—like growing into a deeper relationship with God, spending time with those He has placed in our lives and doing His will.[19]

*NOW, LET'S MEDITATE. REMEMBER:*

- Read the scripture reference 3 times.
- Then meditate on them by allowing any word(s) that stand out to you to repeat in your mind. If your mind wanders, decide to return to the word(s) or the entire scripture.
- Remain meditative until you fully experience the scripture. What is God saying to you? What are you saying to yourself?
- Note your experiences.
- Do NOT jump up out of the meditation and move into "rush" mode. Allow the final minutes of the meditation experience to linger with you. As you meditate daily, the meditation experience will carry you through more and more of your day.

**Read** Genesis 1:26a, 27a, 31.

> "God spoke: 'Let us make human beings in our image, make them reflecting our nature . . .' God created human beings; he created them godlike, reflecting God's nature. He created them male and female . . . God looked over everything he had made; it was so good, so very good! It was evening, it was morning—Day Six." *("THE MESSAGE")*

**Meditate.**
> **Record your experience(s).**
>> **Linger in the ending moments.**
>>> **Carry the ending moments forward into your day.**

## DAY TWO—The Whole Self

The mind is important, but it is only one part of us as human beings. Our essence is spirit, the part of us that most resembles our Creator. Each of us has a soul which develops over time. Our bodies provide a physical "home" for our spirits and souls while supporting our internal and external communication with the world. The following diagram illustrates the connection and interaction between the three expressions of our selves.

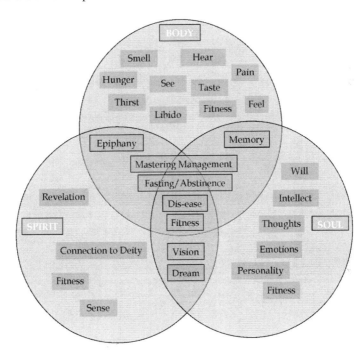

Obviously within the body we have our five senses *(smell, sight, hearing touch, taste)*, our physical drives *(hunger, libido)*, and symptoms to get our attention *(pain, thirst, hunger—physical stimuli that serve more than one purpose)*. Within our soul we have our will, intellect, emotions, and personality. Our spirit includes revelation, our "sixth" sense, and our connection to the Deity. All three expressions have distinct fitness levels. We can have healthy bodies without having healthy souls or spirits.

The diagram illustrates that all three expressions intersect together and there are intersections that only involve two expressions. Between our soul and spirit we experience visions and dreams. Epiphanies bridge our spirits and bodies. Our memory involves our souls and bodies. There are four key experiences that involve our spirits, souls, and bodies. Self-denial *(i.e., fasting, sexual abstinence)* is essential to master self-management. Just as there is a fitness level for each expression of our beings, there is an overall fitness level that is affected by the degree of dis-ease we experience—even allow. *(I'm sure there are other examples of double and triple intersections.)*

To get to peace we have to have balance. Better and better balance within self comes from an acquisition of awareness and then intentional understanding of that which composes our selves. From awareness to intentional understanding to balance we can be peaceful. Therefore, scripturally based meditation becomes *critical* as our minds are strengthened with intelligence, becoming more and more in tune with the knowledge of God.

**Read** John 4:24.
> **Meditate.**
> > **Record your experience(s).**
> > > **Linger in the ending moments.**
> > > > **Carry the ending moments forward into your day.**

## DAY THREE—The Music Factor

Music can enhance the meditation experience.

What is music?

". . . any rhythmic sequence of pleasing sounds."[20]

"Music is the human institution in which individuals create meaning and beauty through sound, using the arts of composition, improvisation, performance and listening."[21]

"A single piece of music, carefully played, can alter the entire atmosphere and behavior in a place."[22] Consider a portion of the story of Saul and David in the 16th chapter of 1 Samuel. Saul was troubled by an "evil spirit." *(The discussion regarding the fact that the evil spirit came from God is for another forum.)* In the 16th verse he was advised to

"'search for someone who can play the harp. He will play when the evil spirit from God comes upon you, and you will feel better.' So Saul said to his attendants, 'Find someone who plays well and bring him to me.'" *(1 Samuel 16:16-17)*

After receiving the recommendation of David, Saul sent for him via a messenger to David's father, Jesse.

"David came to Saul and entered his service. Saul liked him very much, and David became one of his armor-bearers. Then Saul sent word to Jesse, saying, 'Allow David to remain in my service, for I am pleased with him.' Whenever the spirit from God came upon Saul, David would take his harp and play. Then relief would come to Saul; he would feel better, and the evil spirit would leave him." *(1 Samuel 16:21-23)*[23]

"The greatest, most inspiring music speaks to your soul."[24] And that is, again, what we are after, an enlightenment of the soul.

Of course, one person's music can be another person's noise. Beyond style or genre, considering music in Christian meditation, the music must be a tool that will increase our awareness of God's presence and will liberate us to receive revelation and knowledge. Some of my musician friends find music distracting as they hear the technicalities of the piece. For them silence may be music to their ears.

Choose what works for you.

**Read** Psalm 92:1-2.
    **Meditate.**
        **Record your experience(s).**
            **Linger in the ending moments.**
                **Carry the ending moments forward into your day.**

## DAY FOUR—*Effort, Enlightening, Empowering*

How has it been so far? Are you finding meditation simple, but certainly, not easy?

### EFFORT

For most of us, we need effort and discipline to meditate, simply because, we are not inclined to do so, naturally. Or there are circumstances that we consider too powerful to overcome in order to make meditation a part of our lives:

- waking up *and getting up* in enough time to meditate and still be on time for our day's obligations, or
- the ability to sit still, or
- choosing not to use the time to make "to do" lists.

These "forces . . . are so strong," and seemingly, disconnected from our need to change "that an inner commitment and a certain kind of work are necessary," to keep up with our decision to capture life's moments.[25] Remember, capturing life's moments is one benefit of meditation. It keeps us "in touch with many aspects of our lives that are habitually, overlooked, and lost to us."[26]

### ENLIGHTENING

How often did our elders remind us that "anything worth having is worth working for?" The work of meditation may be just that—*work*, but the benefits far outweigh our sacrifice(s). We've already discussed one advantage—not missing life's moments. Other benefits include becoming enlightened, which leads to liberation; and liberation leads to utter freedom. We begin to "see more clearly and understand more deeply."[27] This is not always painless. We may enter areas of hidden pain and grief as well as joy and peace. That's why we really have *to prepare* to prepare to enter into meditative experiences. We have to go through temporary discomfort to heal, in order to live in increased wholeness. Ignoring the cause of pain or discomfort or grief never causes it to go away or decrease. Disregarding pain only delays an eventual confrontation; and delay usually increases the intensity of the situation.

Meditation "is liberating in that it leads to new ways of being in" ourselves and in our relationships.[28] It frees us from the places in which we get stuck or weighed down, not allowing us to move onward and upward with our lives.

## EMPOWERING

When we meditate, our revelations empower us. "Knowledge is power." From revelation to knowledge we grow in strength and ability to be and become all of who we were created to be. In these quiet, intentional times, we learn more about the seeds of dreams and deposits of fortitude and "lay-a-ways" of gifts that God has placed within us. These are the treasures that we have been too busy or too distracted to notice—because we would not be still.

Therefore, we are empowered to make better choices. We are empowered to answer the following questions—even if the answers frighten us a bit: Who am I? Why am I? How am I . . . ? When am I . . . ?

**Read** John 1:1.
    **Meditate.**
        **Record your experience(s).**
            **Linger in the ending moments.**
                **Carry the ending moments forward into your day.**

## DAY FIVE—*Revisiting Purpose*

As a young woman I never wrestled with the notion of living in a big world. For, I did not even know I had a unique place in this seemingly vast universe. I did, however, know I had a place within certain institutions—family, schools, churches, the workplace, etc. In turn, I believed that these institutions had a certain position in the world. My connection to the world had to be through, or because of, an institution. I didn't have enough sense of my selfhood at the time to know that I, as an individual, had my own position—not needing an association with a credible group. That very concept was overwhelming.

The night I understood my individual position in the world is one I will never forget. This revelation occurred as I had a vision while praying with a friend. I saw the world as a vast, lush green field with blades of grass waving in the wind. Clearly I saw a place for me to stand, a tiny clearing that would accommodate only my feet. There was a place for me—just for me. No one else could fill that spot. God created that spot just for me and created me just for that spot. "'For I know the plans I have for you,' declares the Lord, 'plans to prosper you and not to harm you, plans to give you hope and a future.'" *(Jeremiah 29:11)*

I must add here, that this realization of being an important individual in the universe does not mean that we are called to our journeys alone. We are called to be in relationship with others, to support and to be supported. In tandem, we hold sacred the importance of our individual contributions. The "place" just would not be the same without any one of us!

Have you ever considered what the Bible would be like without certain characters? Have you ever wondered how differently the story would have turned out without a snake, a Pharaoh, or a Herod? Or what if the character remained in the story, but she or he was just a little better at this or that? What if Adam didn't take Eve's word for it? What if Jacob was more honest? What if Judas was more courageous and wasn't tempted by fast cash?

I've heard that heroic people have heroic flaws. Also, I heard a preacher pray that his success would never outpace the strength of his character. Until recently, I was not able to give true credit to the flaws of biblical characters. Until recently, I could not appreciate the purposes served by them. Yes, even their flaws had purpose. And ahhh, if their flaws had a purpose, maybe my flaws serve a purpose as well. Just as God worked through those human beings, those vessels of clay who were just as flawed as I am—or more so—likewise, God will work through me.

The Vessel
*(Author Unknown)*

"The Master was picking a vessel to use; on His shelves there were many—which one would He choose?

'Take me,' cried the gold one, 'I'm shiny and bright. I am of great value. I do things just right. My beauty and luster will outshine the rest. For someone like You, Master, gold would be best!'

The Master passed on, with no word at all. He looked at a silver urn, narrow and tall. 'I'll serve You, dear Master. I'll pour out Your wine. I'll be at Your table whenever You dine. My lines are so graceful; my carvings so true, the silver I'm made of will compliment You.'

Unheeding, the Master passed on to the brass. It was wide-mouthed and shallow and polished like glass. 'Here! Here!,' cried the vessel, 'I know I will do. Place me on Your table for all men to view.'

'Look at me,' called the goblet of crystal so clear. 'My transparency shows my contents are quite dear. Although I am fragile, I will serve You with pride. I am sure I'll be happy in Your house to abide.'

The Master came next to a vessel of wood, polished and carved, it solidly stood. 'You may use me, dear Master,' the wooden bowl said, 'But I'd rather You used me for fruit, not for bread!'

Then the Master looked down, saw a vessel of clay. It was empty and broken where it helplessly lay. No hope had the vessel, the Master might choose, to cleanse it, to fill it, make it whole, fit for use.

'Ah!,' said the Master. 'This vessel I choose. I will mend it and fill it and put it to use. I need not the vessel with pride in itself, nor the one who is narrow to sit on the shelf, nor the one who is big-mouthed and shallow and loud, nor the one who displays his contents so proud, nor the one who thinks he can do all things just right—but this plain earthy vessel filled with my power and might.

He then gently lifted the vessel of clay, to mend it and cleanse it. He filled it that day. He spoke to it kindly, 'There's work you must do. Just pour out to others as I pour into you.'

Paul wrote Timothy:
'But in a great house there are not only vessels of gold and of silver, but also of wood and of earth; and some to honour, and some to dishonour. If a man; therefore, purge himself from these, he shall be a vessel unto honour, sanctified and meet for the master's use, and prepared unto every good work.' (2 Timothy 2:20-21, KJV)"

What problem did you come to solve? What is your purpose? Do you believe God to accomplish it through you?

**Read** Psalm 57:2.
> **Meditate.**
> > **Record your experience(s).**
> > > **Linger in the ending moments.**
> > > > **Carry the ending moments forward into your day.**

## DAY SIX—*Standing in the Wind, Riding the Waves*

Many people think of the beach, with its view of the ocean, as an ideal location to relax oneself via meditation. I wonder how many of these people have ever compared the waves of an ocean to the "waves" in their minds. What about you? No doubt most of us would contrast these two concepts rather than parallel them.

However, we can gain greater understanding of how meditation works by considering the surface of an ocean, or even a lake. "There are always waves on the water. Sometimes they are big; sometimes they are small; and sometimes they are almost imperceptible."[29] Yet they are always present. "The water's waves are churned up by winds which come and go and vary in direction and intensity, just as do the winds of stress and change in our lives, which stir up waves in our minds."[30]

So with the winds and the waves in our minds, how can there be peace?

Certainly, meditation, contrary to some schools of thought, is not a manipulative mechanism by which we trick ourselves into believing that everything is all right when it is not. Remember, you have *to prepare* to prepare for meditation, because you will encounter, sooner or later, something uncomfortable. Meditation brings you in contact with a "realer" reality and a truer truth—yet—there is peace.

Peace comes from acknowledging reality and truth. Then through meditation, learning "how to work with it . . . 'you can't stop the waves, but you can learn to surf.'"[31] Have you ever heard that the calmest place in a storm is in its center, in its eye?

> "Peace. It does not mean to be in a place where there is no noise, trouble or hard work. It means to be in the midst of those things and still be calm in your heart."[32]

Surfing can be making your way to the center until the winds die down and the storm passes over. And, it will certainly pass over; it didn't come to stay. We are in a constant state of motion. The earth revolves on its axis and orbits around the sun. Seasons change every few months. Whatever the wind is in your life, it didn't come to stay.

Surfing can also be speaking to the storm—taking authority over it. Do you remember the story when the disciples were on the boat and a storm arose? The winds were causing the waves to toss the boat to and fro. The disciples became scared and wondered why Jesus, their leader, their protector, was asleep so peacefully in the back of the boat *and* on a cushion, no less? His peace caused them more unrest than the storm itself. "Frantically they woke him up, shouting, 'Teacher, don't you even care that we are going to drown?'"[33]

My guess is that Jesus was having a necessary, quite pleasant moment of rest on his cushion—maybe even enjoying a good dream—and they woke him, because of a few waves rising up on a lake! Remember he was there when the expanse was created to separate the water above from the water below. He was there when the oceans were formed. *(Genesis 1:7)* Yet, he responded to them by waking and speaking peace to the wind, thus calming their fears—at least for the moment.

"You ain't know?"—Jesus possibly wanted to ask them. "You ain't know you could tell the wind to stop blowing and it would obey because you have authority over it?"

How often have you witnessed others in a state of serenity, not in denial, but truly in a peaceful state during some of the most devastating circumstances in their lives? Were you staring at them in disbelief? Were you asking, "How can you be so calm? You must not be aware of what *really* is going on!"

Did they simply reply, "Yes, I am aware. You ain't know?"

**Read** Psalm 131:2.
**Meditate.**
**Record your experience(s).**
**Linger in the ending moments.**
**Carry the ending moments forward into your day.**

## DAY SEVEN—*Journey* . . .

> *"In the middle of this road we call our life*
> *I found myself in a dark wood*
> *With no clear path through."*[34]

We often compare the process of life to that of taking a journey. And, just like any journey to unknown destinations, we may frequently ask the questions, "Are we there yet? How much longer?" Regarding our lives, we inquire more specifically:

- Are we ever going to arrive?
- Arrive where? Just arrive.
- Will we ever accumulate enough secure wealth never to worry about resources?
- Will we ever have enough variety in our closets never to spend 20 minutes trying to remember the last time we wore a certain outfit?
- It's our fourth child; will we ever figure out how to parent without drama?
- Will we ever purchase a house with enough space?
- Will we ever drive our dream cars?
- Will we ever learn?
- Just once, may we complete a project without everything going wrong?

Will we ever arrive . . . at our desired destinations?

Since we are trying so hard to get to the destinations as soon as we can, our perspectives on life are skewed, and we accumulate unnecessary worry, stress, and anxiety. *(We will discuss this more in the next chapter.)* Not only do we worry about when we'll get there, we stress over the "obstacles in the way." Are they obstacles or opportunities? Are they there to be in the way, blocking us, or to slow us down so we gain more knowledge as we go along?

> Stop your frantic push for success. Take time to *taste the present.*
> The fires of desire will *always* rage within you. You must dominate
> that rage and focus it. *Learn to rest.*[35]

We are going too fast, missing lessons to be learned and moments to be enjoyed. "When we practice meditation, we are really acknowledging that in this moment, we are on the road of life. The path unfolds in this moment and in every moment while we are alive."[36]

Now exactly how can we proceed, knowing and seeing challenges—big ones—without concern about how well we will make it through them? Jesus was the answer to this question for His disciples while He was on earth. Just because the disciples often did not reach a level of rest from Jesus' teachings *(as we read yesterday)*, does not mean that we cannot today.

Today we have access to God in ways that believers did not in Jesus' time. Since Jesus fulfilled his purpose *(life, death, and resurrection)*, the entire universe not only has access to salvation, the entire universe has access to living a best life. This is our individual and collective best life—for ourselves and our environment. Will we seek rest in God's Presence or will we be like the disciples and yield to fear?

It's always our choice.

**Read** Luke 9:3.
> **Meditate.**
>> **Record your experience(s).**
>>> **Linger in the ending moments.**
>>>> **Carry the ending moments forward into your day.**

# *three*

## *eternity*

*As I write this now, I wish I could tell you that something profound happened to change my life at that time of seeking God. Nothing deep happened. I trudged on, somehow forgetting that I had all these questions. I met a young man that I ended up marrying after graduation. He was majoring in advertising; so, I majored in public relations. He met a retail industry recruiter one day on campus; so, I accompanied him to a mixer for the free food, and we both ended up being hired by two major retail chains, respectively. We moved to my hometown and were married within one month. Eight months later, I was pregnant. Three months after that, I was unemployed—and moving into a larger apartment. After giving birth to a beautiful, healthy baby girl, the feelings I thought I'd forgotten began to resurface. But, this time, they were more robust. This time they came with a few more years of hurts, disappointments, and pain. The trap of a limited perspective was tightening its grip.*

*Particularly pressing during this time was my inability to feel worthy—of even living. I did not know how to feel worthy when I was not working and contributing to our household. I did not know how to feel worthy remembering that I did not succeed at my first job out of college. I did not know how to feel worthy when I felt so empty. I remember, briefly, considering suicide. I did not believe I had anything to offer.*

*Unworthy. Empty. Failure.*

*One night, as I lay curled up in a ball on the bed, my husband reminded me of the precious life in the next room, a sweet little girl who was depending on me. Only I could give her some of the things she would need in this life. And, for my birthday that year, he tossed a journal into my lap. He challenged, "You say you're a writer. So write."*

*week two*

## DAY ONE—*Chasing the Wind*

Remember the list of questions from chapter one? I have another one. If God is sovereign—why do we even ask?

> "He has made everything beautiful in its time. He has also set eternity in the hearts of men; yet they cannot fathom what God has done from beginning to end." (Ecclesiastes 3:11b, c)

The planting of the seed of eternity causes us to ask questions, to ponder infinite issues. We ponder and we ask even when we know that the reality of our finiteness limits our ability to comprehend the answers fully.

However, since we have this seed in us, we cannot help ourselves. There is a part of us that knows there is more. No matter how much we accomplish by either temporal or eternal standards—there is always a tugging for more. Too many of us respond too often to this tugging in the wrong way. We respond with striving for more accomplishments for the sake of accomplishing more. Then we may get to a point where we are even more accomplished—and still, there is a tugging. We continue to probe, asking the deeper questions just like the author of Ecclesiastes.

> "What does man gain from all his labor at which he toils under the sun?" *(Ecclesiastes 1:3)*

> ". . . wisdom is better than folly" but "the fate of the fool will overtake me also. What then do I gain by being wise?" *(Ecclesiastes 2:13a, 15b, c)*

Or, just like the rich young ruler in Mark 10, verse 17 reads, "Good teacher," he asked [Jesus], 'what must I do to inherit eternal life?'" Jesus challenged him to leave behind all that was temporal—the Law, his status, his wealth. Give it up and declare it unimportant. The young man did not stick around to hear the rest of the story, as Jesus conveyed to Peter in verses 29-30:

> "I tell you the truth," Jesus replied, "no one who has left home or brothers or sisters or mother or father or children or fields for me and the gospel will fail to receive a hundred times as much *in this present age* (homes, brothers, sisters, mothers, children, and fields—and with them persecutions) and in the age to come, eternal life." *[Author's emphasis.]*

Or, consider the other side of the spectrum—those who are ostracized from the mainstream of society like the Samaritan woman who met Jesus at the well. *(John 4:4-26, 39-42)* Jesus explains that the water she draws from the well will leave her thirsty again. However, if she or anyone else were to drink of the timeless water He had to offer, "indeed, the water I give him will become in him a spring of water welling up to eternal life."[37] She accepted His offer of *His* kind of water so that she would not have to return to *that* well again. Now that she would not have to return to it, she also would no longer face a reminder of how she did not fit in. No longer would she have to go to a place that reminded her of her limitations that kept her in a steady state of regret and shame.

Whether we are like the wisest king in the world, the richest ruler, or the thirstiest woman in town—our living with only a focus on the physical will always lead us to a "bottom experience." We will hit "rock bottom," a very dry place, where all we can, vaguely, sense is the existence of the seed planted in us long ago. It has never stopped tugging, even when the other things in our lives desensitized us from perceiving it. It has never stopped tugging, even when we ignored it. So now that we are at the bottom and we sense it—even more than before—we must satisfy the tugging.

The only way to do so is to go to its source.

*Let us add an intentional awareness of breathing with our meditation this week.*

*Let us be aware of the rhythm of our breathing.*
*(You may either inhale and exhale through your nose—or—inhale through your nose and exhale through your mouth—whichever flows best.)*

*As we move into our day, we should allow ourselves to return to our meditative experience and remember the breathing as a tool to return to the peaceful state of the ending moments.*

**Read** Ecclesiastes 3:11.
> **Meditate, aware of inhaling and exhaling deeply.**
>> **Record your experience(s).**
>>> **Linger in the ending moments.**
>>>> **Carry the ending moments forward into your day.**

## DAY TWO—The Eternity Seed

What is eternity? What is the seed that has been planted in us? What is eternity?

A better question actually is—Who is eternity? Of course the answer is God. Recall Ecclesiastes 3:11b, c: "He has also set eternity in the hearts of men; yet they cannot fathom what God has done from beginning to end."

Now let's look at Revelation 1:8:

> "'I am the Alpha and the Omega,' says the Lord God, 'who is, and who was, and who is to come, the Almighty."

And Revelation 1:11:

> "Saying, 'I am Alpha and Omega, the first and the last: . . .'" (KJV)

And Revelation 21:6:

> "He said to me: 'It is done. I am the Alpha and the Omega, the Beginning and the End . . .'"

And Revelation 22:13

> "'I am the Alpha and the Omega, the First and the Last, the Beginning and the End . . .'"

It seems to me that being the Beginning and the End, God is Eternity. **It is God, which God has set in the hearts of human beings!**

Let's consider Genesis 1:26, 27:

> "Then God said, 'Let us make man in our image, in our likeness, . . . 'So God created man in his own image, in the image of God he created him; male and female he created them.'"

And Genesis 2:7:

> "The Lord God formed the man from the dust of the ground and breathed into his nostrils the breath of life, and the man became a living being."

Just like we have physical and other traits from our physical parents, because they procreated us, we have an eternal trait from God, our Creator. When God created us, God set eternity in our hearts.

Let's look deeper at the meanings of the key words of Ecclesiastes 3:11: set, eternity, and heart.

> **Set**—in Hebrew the word is *nathan* (pronounced naw-than). This word can mean a lot of different things. Among the meanings are: give, put, make, add, apply, appoint, ascribe, bestow, bring, cast, cause, commit, distribute, fasten, leave, ordain, render.

> **Eternity**—in Hebrew the word is *olam* (pronounced o-lawm). This word means concealed, i.e., the vanishing point. Generally *olam* is time out of mind, past or future, i.e., practically eternity, without end.

> **Heart**—in Hebrew the word is *leb* (pronounced labe). This word is used figuratively, very widely, for the feelings, the will, and even the intellect. It is the center of anything. (*Leb* is a form of *lebab* (pronounced lay-bawb}. This word means the most center organ.)

Now let's rewrite the verse. **"God has fastened time that is out of my mind, time that I cannot comprehend with my intellect alone, in the center of my being."**

As you meditate, consider a question asked by many of us at different parts of our lives, "Who am I really?"

**Read** Genesis 1:26, 27.
> **Meditate, aware of inhaling and exhaling deeply.**
> > **Record your experience(s).**
> > > **Linger in the ending moments.**
> > > > **Carry the ending moments forward into your day.**

## DAY THREE—*Beyond What We Can Fathom*

No wonder we ask questions. As we considered in the previous chapter, we know there is something more, much more than we can comprehend. The fact that we cannot comprehend does not keep us from asking. While we cannot comprehend, we have the potential to do so because what we cannot comprehend has been fastened in our souls. That is what keeps us seeking. Robert Browning wrote, "A man's reach should exceed his grasp, or what is a heaven for?" Another similar, and maybe a more familiar saying is, "If you shoot for the moon, you'll land among the stars."

Our questions are fine, even beneficial, but focusing on them can bring about stress and anxiety. Concentrating constantly on what, when, where, how, and why can cause us to go 'round and 'round in circles. Concentrating constantly on questions distracts you from "keeping the main thing, the main thing." Concentrating constantly on questions elevates the situation above God. Concentrating constantly on the questions keeps you from acquiring an eternal perspective. This perspective is much more than filtering out what is unimportant. This perspective is seeing as God sees. This perspective is living out eternity while existing in the temporal.

Ask your questions, but let them lead you to a deeper, more intimate relationship with God. Ask your questions, but let them lead you to a greater understanding of the universe and who you are—who you really are.

**Read** John 15:7.
> **Meditate, aware of inhaling and exhaling deeply.**
> > **Record your experience(s).**
> > > **Linger in the ending moments.**
> > > > **Carry the ending moments forward into your day.**

## DAY FOUR—*Evidence of the Eternal or Temporal*

What questions do you ask of God? What kinds of petitions are a part of your prayers?

Stop now, and if you write down your questions/petitions in your journal, review them. If you do not, currently, record your questions/petitions, make a list of the kinds of things that are a part of your questions/petitions.

_____

Now, are these temporal or eternal matters? Are these issues of this physical world or are these issues concerning the spiritual world?

In the 12th chapter of the Gospel of Luke, Jesus tells a parable about a rich fool *(verses 13-21)*. Throughout the parable, Jesus is responding to a request from someone in the crowd regarding the inheritance he wants to share with his brother. From the story, Jesus instructs the man that he can be successful in acquiring those things (money, possessions) which will free him from worry over physical needs, but at the same time as soon as he acquires these things, he can be called home by God. Then, in the end, what good are his acquisitions?

The Teacher in Ecclesiastes exhibits a similar concern over his work on earth in the 2nd chapter, verses 17-21b:

> "So I hated life, . . . I hated all things I had toiled for under the sun, because I must leave them to the one who comes after me. And who knows whether he will be a wise man or a fool? Yet he will have control over all the work in which I have poured my effort and skill under the sun . . . So my heart began to despair over all my toilsome labor under the sun. For a man may do his work with wisdom, knowledge, and skill, and then he must leave all he owns to someone who has not worked for it."

Now, back to Luke 12—after Jesus ministers to the people via the parable, He "said to His disciples: 'Therefore I tell you, do not worry about your life, what you will eat; or about your body, what you will wear. Life is more than food, and the body more than clothes.'" *(verses 22, 23)* Jesus declares that God takes *good* care of the animals that cannot store up provisions and we are more valuable to God than the animals. Therefore, will not God provide for us, as valuable as we are to God?

Moreover, Jesus asks in verses 25 and 26, "'Who of you by worrying can add a single hour to his life? Since you cannot do this very little thing, why do you worry about the rest?'" What is the important thing here? How long you live on this earth—how many chances you have to fulfill your purpose—is much more important than what you eat and wear; and you cannot affect even that! *That* is something about which to be concerned. Since God has this "big thing" covered, surely God's covered the "little stuff" as well.

> "" . . ., You have such little faith! Don't keep worrying about having something to eat or drink. Only people who don't know God are always worrying about such things. Your Father knows what you need. But put God's work first, and these things will be yours as well."" *(Luke 12:28c-31, Contemporary English Version)*

Ahhhh, so it is a matter of faith.

Do you have confidence, trust, and belief that God will take care of your needs? Do you have faith that you will have what you need when you need it? Of all the questions that we can ask which cause us stress and anxiety, I believe the top two are **when** and **why**, in that order. We can handle the what, how, how much, etc., if we just know when it would happen. Yet, time is in God's hand. I heard a preacher declare that we can pray, but God is not our "errand boy." God will answer. God will show up in God's time, which, of course, is the perfect time. God's timing is not subjected to what we perceive to be the right time. Faith says, "Circumstantial time has run out on my need. Yet I know that God's got it." Now that's an eternal perspective!

As you prepare to meditate, consider what the Word of God advises about the questions you should ask, the petitions you should pray.

**Read** Luke 12:22, 23.
> **Meditate, aware of inhaling and exhaling deeply.**
> > **Record your experience(s).**
> > > **Linger in the ending moments.**
> > > > **Carry the ending moments forward into your day.**

## DAY FIVE—Eternity Is Now

It should be obvious to us, since a piece of eternity is grafted to our beings, but it is not.

We do not have to wait until our bodies die to experience eternity. We can experience eternity right now—as long as we choose to live with an eternal perspective. Do you recall Jesus' words to Peter from Day One's reading? ". . . no one . . . will fail to receive a hundred times as much *in this present age* . . ." Not one person who gives up any worldly asset for the sake of focusing on spiritual matters will fail to gain a significant return of worldly assets. Eternity is now.

"Life is more than food and the body more than clothes." *(Luke 12:23)*

Let us be true to who we are, really. Let's not unduly clutter our time with God and with ourselves and with each other by focusing on temporal, material matters of food, clothing, shelter, bills, etc. Rather, let us experience being . . . be-ing.

So then, what do we talk with God about? If we believe our basic needs are handled, then what's left to pray about? These questions remind me of those oft-asked by couples who have been together a number of years. If we don't talk about our finances or our business or our children or our aging parents, what's left to talk about or do? When we get here, we know we have lost our intimacy with our loved one. I hope we have discovered by this day in the journey that meditation creates/restores intimacy with God and with ourselves.

"Life is more than food and the body more than clothes."

Let's consider the prayer of Jabez as an example of an alternative to routine, provision-based communication.

> "Jabez cried out to the God of Israel, 'Oh that you would bless me and enlarge my territory! Let your hand be with me, and keep me from harm so that I will be free from pain.' And God granted his request." *(1 Chronicles 4:10)*

Jabez cried out. He did not mumble a prayer. Impassioned, Jabez prayed for a deeper experience of God. This was not a prayer for more money or a bigger house. Rather, Jabez knew the physical limitations into which he was born and prayed that God would "flip the script." Jabez prayed for deliverance from the curse of being associated with pain *(the meaning of his name)*. Jabez wanted more of eternity.

Let's not waste time and energy focusing on money, cars, houses or even love interests. Let's ask for the deeper things of God, for the generational curses to die with us, for understanding of our purpose, indeed—for enlarged borders.

When we seek out larger territories and dare to walk with the giants in the promised lands, we have tapped into who God is and who we are. We begin to act in ways that confirm our knowledge that we come from eternity and that with God, nothing is impossible.

**Read** 1 Chronicles 4:10 three (3) times.
    **Meditate, aware of inhaling and exhaling deeply.**
        **Record your experience(s).**
            **Linger in the ending moments.**
                **Carry the ending moments forward into your day.**

## DAY SIX—Border Bustin'

The concept of territory, of borders is an important one as we attempt to acquire an eternal perspective on life.

Merriam-Webster defines territory as an assigned area and border as a boundary. Looking at the Hebrew word for this concept, *gbul* (pronounced gheb-ool). It means a boundary or a limit that encloses a territory.

So, a border designates what your assigned area is. Notwithstanding his physical circumstances into which he was born, Jabez had a grasp on an eternal perspective that caused him to cry out to God to change those physical circumstances, to enlarge the area to which he was assigned.

We can look at what we see with our physical eye and let that limit our lives. *Or*, we can reach for *and* grasp an eternal perspective and realize that we are made in the image of God, the Eternal One, and believe that there is more because we have eternity fastened to our soul.

I contend that it was not David's praise that made him a man after God's own heart. If we remember the physical circumstances into which David was born, they were not all that different from Jabez's circumstances. David, too, was at a disadvantage. He was not considered to be as physically appealing as his brothers. His brothers better fit the image the Israelites had of a king, reminiscent of the Cinderella fairy tale. Yet, the anointing oil did not flow over them. Samuel, the prophet God sent to anoint the king who would follow Saul, knew he precisely needed the man over which the oil would flow. Upon Samuel's insistent questioning of whether more sons existed, Jesse, David's father, finally pointed Samuel toward the field. God had God's treasure "hidden" in the field, tending the sheep—David.

Yet, even when David received the anointing to be king, he had to fight while living in exile before he acquired the authority to be king. More than David's praise, which made him a man after God's own heart, it was David's walking with God as God enlarged his territory. Then because David knew so well who God was and who he was in God, he praised God so. David dared to walk with God. David dared to walk with Eternity.

2 Corinthians 3:18 describes our spiritual maturation process as one of going from glory to glory. As we grow and seek ascent from level of glory to another, we cannot forget that there are boundaries that demark each territory of glory. There are borders. Crossing them is not always easy; in fact, most of the time, crossing a border that leads to increase is usually challenging. In her ending sermon during a fall revival at Ben Hill United Methodist Church *(Atlanta, GA)*, Rev. Dr. Alfreda Wiggins identified the forces that attempt to keep us from crossing these borders. She called them "border bullies." Though they exist, we cannot allow them to keep us from our growth.

In the 17th chapter of Luke, we find a story of 10 lepers whom Jesus met "as he traveled 'along the border between Samaria and Galilee.'"[38] While Jesus met them on the border between two cities, he also met them along the invisible border between "isolation and the return to society."[39]

> "Everyone at some point comes to a border. That border may be the end of our strength, our ability, our intellect, our health, or our life span. But whenever or wherever we encounter a border, Christ helps us by means we may not understand . . . Jesus walks at our life's borders."[40]

If we cannot answer the question of who we really are, then we are stuck with what we see, hear, taste, smell, and feel physically. We will stay within our "assigned area," never gaining an eternal perspective.

**Read** 1 Chronicles 4:10.

**Meditate, aware of inhaling and exhaling deeply.**

**Record your experience(s).**

**Linger in the ending moments.**

**Carry the ending moments forward into your day.**

## DAY SEVEN—Walk . . . and Pray

So now, I pray that we have decided to gain an eternal perspective. This means that we are actually sensing the eternity that is in our souls. We are abiding in Christ, believing God for the expanded territory. We have decided to overcome obstacles; and we are determined to slay some giants. We are walking confidently, prepared to enter Job-like *(unfathomable)* experiences when they occur.

Once we enter the experience, how do we live within it? If we should not focus on questions of when and why and not focus on the physical circumstances, what are we to do? Pauline scriptures provide some insight:

> "Do not be anxious about anything, but in everything, by prayer and petition, with thanksgiving, present your requests to God. And the peace of God, which transcends all understanding, will guard your hearts and your minds in Christ Jesus." (Philippians 4:6, 7)

First, we reaffirm our commitment to ourselves and God that we will not worry. We replace worry with intimate communication. With thanksgiving, we let God know what hurts. With thanksgiving, we share our feelings. With thanksgiving, we let God know that we are not enjoying this situation—yet our answer is still "yes," still deciding to follow God, no matter what challenges we experience. Then we leave the situation with God, living within a peace that others may not understand, continuing to walk forward toward our eternal goals.

The border bullies exist to impede progress, while simultaneously testing our perseverance.

- Do we really believe what we have claimed?
- Do we really desire to arrive at our eternal destinations?
- How serious are we about living with an eternal perspective?

When times are particularly challenging for me, living out my purpose, the passage that Paul wrote in 2 Corinthians 4, strongly, encourages my heart.

> "Therefore, since through God's mercy, we have this ministry, we do not lose heart . . . We are hard pressed on every side, but not crushed; perplexed, but not in despair; persecuted, but not abandoned; struck down, but not destroyed." (verses 1, 8, 9)

Paul's exhortation in the fifth chapter of Romans is also powerful:

> "And we rejoice in the hope of the glory of God. Not only so, but we also rejoice in our sufferings, because we know that suffering produces perseverance; perseverance, character; and character, hope. And hope does not disappoint us . . ." (verses 2-5)

**Read** either of the excerpted Scriptures as printed above from Philippians 4:6,7; 2 Corinthians 4:1,8,9; or Romans 5:2-5.

**Meditate, aware of inhaling and exhaling deeply.**

**Record your experience(s).**

**Linger in the ending moments.**

**Carry the ending moments forward into your day.**

# *four*

## *inside*

*Wow—I had not written anything, even a journal entry, in about two years. Putting pen to paper then, I felt like a kindergartener tracing over pre-printed dashed letters with a dull pencil on that horribly rough manila paper with flecks of red and blue in it. Write about what? Anything; just write. So I did. Then several things happened to rejuvenate my soul.*

*I discovered a support network at a local temporary agency which reaffirmed my abilities, placing me at an entry-level job where I excelled. I was greatly inspired to dream again from reading Susan Taylor's* In the Spirit *and Alex Haley's* Autobiography of Malcolm X. *And, of course, I found God again at a dynamically, spiritually diverse protestant church.*

*Yet, as I flourished, my marriage floundered. Funny how the gift led me on a path away from the gift-giver. I was becoming more of the real me and as one might imagine, that was not the person my husband married. In the end, our separation was a relief to both of us. We had a great courtship and we have remained solid friends since our divorce. We simply should not have married.*

*week three*

## DAY ONE—*More on My Dry Place*

Some people describe the unworthy feelings I felt as empty. That is not what I experienced. I was not empty. I was dry. "Stuff" existed within me, but it was not watered. And, as the winds of life blew upon my "stuff dust," and as the "stuff dust particles" blew away, part of me went with them.

I was almost 24 years old and had trouble recalling anything in my history to help me deal with my dryness. Actually, there was plenty of history, but I had covered it up with layers upon layers of too much loveless sex and too much drinking. Finally, I had gotten married—just 'cause he asked me, and I did not want to move back home with my family after college graduation. Now, the "stuff dust" was settled. The "stuff dust" was no longer being watered; therefore, it was drying up. I was drying up. I was married, but I was not fulfilling my destiny. I was so incredibly thirsty.

The water which replenished my "stuff dust" was water like that which the Samaritan woman drew from the well in John 4. It kept me coming back for more. The kind of water I received when I was writing. When I wrote, I was fulfilling my destiny. The problem was that I had not chosen writing as a career. Instead, I had chosen a career path that I believed would lead me to quicker financial success.

Anyway, I share this part of my story to convey that prior to recommitting to a church family, I was not pursuing an intimate relationship with God. Like in college, I recited some kind of prayer each night before going to sleep. I attempted to read a bit of the Bible now and then, but nothing was making a whole lot of sense, even with The New Living Translation. Yet, there was a part of me beyond my control. There was a part that was seeking to be fulfilled, to be watered. Could it have been the Eternity that was fastened to my soul?

*Let us add moderate movement with our meditation this week.*

*Gently swaying our arms, moving our heads from side to side, or rotating our feet are all examples of moderate movement while seated.*

*Standing, we could also sway our hips, slowly rise/fall on the balls of our feet, etc.*

*As we move into our day, we should allow ourselves to return
to our meditative experience and remember the movement
as a tool to return to the peaceful state of the ending moments.*

**Read** Psalm 42.

    **Meditate with movement.**

        **Record your experience(s).**

            **Linger in the ending moments.**

                **Carry the ending moments forward into your day.**

## *DAY TWO—The Beginning of Revival*

I've mentioned Susan Taylor's book as pivotal in my spiritual revival. Let me tell you more about the day I met her and bought her book.

To understand my sense of desperation on that day in Atlanta in 1993, you have to understand me. I am not an impulsive person, regularly. Though my husband was quite spontaneous, his temperament was not tolerant. He only seemed spontaneous when the impulse was his. If it were *my* impulse, he became annoyed with having to rearrange his schedule. Additionally, I regularly believed I did not have the money to do the things I liked to do, especially if I had not budgeted for it. And you have to understand that I did not like to enter social situations alone.

So, there I was, deciding on the spot that I needed to be wherever Susan Taylor was going to be that night. I called my husband, with the confidence that he would say yes with no flack—and even if he did say something, I had my comebacks ready. I did not care how much the ticket was or that I would have to buy a book, probably a more expensive hardback edition. See, I needed to purchase a book, because I needed her autograph. I did not even care that it was probably too late to get someone to go with me. In fact, I preferred to be alone. I knew that whatever I was going to get, it was for me, and I was determined to get it—and get it that night.

When I arrived, I found a seat near where she would be. I settled in with an expectant peace that would not be disappointed. I knew I was in the right place at the right time. Later, when Susan Taylor arrived, I said to myself, "I want to be like her. I want for myself what she has." I was not talking about her physical appearance or her commercial success. She had a sense of living a fulfilled life. She had a sense of solid peace. She was full of joy *and* happiness. She was cool. I saw that, and that was what I wanted.

Over the years I have recognized these same qualities in others, women and men alike. When I see it, I step up the drive in myself to go higher in it. These women and men walk as if they are floating. Their smiles are a consistent part of their demeanor. They personify "cool." Part of achieving this "coolness," this peace, comes from chronological age. The older we get, the less we care about what others think, close loved ones or not. *(What we think about what others will think/do in response to what we think/do causes much of our not doing what we desire in our heart of hearts.)* Yet, as God-believers, we do not have to wait until we are senior citizens to live as cool people. We simply need to live from the inside out.

**Read** Philippians 4:4-7. Ponder—what are the things you can do to access a peace that transcends human understanding? Of those things, which one could stand some improvement? Choose the verse that speaks to you with your answers in mind.

**Meditate with movement.**

**Record your experience(s).**

**Linger in the ending moments.**

**Carry the ending moments forward into your day.**

## DAY THREE—*Meeting God at My Ash Tray Level*

Attending the autograph session for Susan Taylor was the beginning of my return to an intimate relationship with God. While I received replenishment at a well that night, I soon discovered that I needed a deeper well from which I could draw. That is where my church membership benefitted me.

While this is where I ended up, God met me where I was to bring me, where I needed to be. In fact, this is how God continues to deal with me. This is how God deals with all of us. God meets us where we are—without condemnation—and leads us to places we never thought we would go.

Theologian Howard Thurman calls this process meeting someone at the "ash tray level."

> "This preliminary residue of God-meaning, however it may be defined, is the starting point of communication between the two principals in the religious experience. It is at this point that the meaning of the experience takes hold. Initially, it cannot be more than this or it would be meaningless; it cannot be less than this or it would be utterly unworthy."[41]

> "There must be a conscious 'toe-hold' for God in religious experience. A friend of mine was having great difficulty because he could not establish any authentic basis of communication with his landlady. He observed one day that her idea of a gentleman was one who kept the ash trays empty of cigarettes and dead matches. He resolved to keep his ash trays empty not only in his own room, but also to make a habit of emptying ash trays wherever he saw that they needed emptying, whenever he came through the living room. It worked like magic—a basis of communication was established now which eventually led to understanding at many levels of appreciation. *He met her at the level of the ash trays.* In religious experience God meets the individual at the level not only of the individual's needs, but also, in my judgment, more incisively, at the level of his residue of God-meaning and goes forward from there."[42]

God sees more of us than we see of ourselves. The saying goes, "He looked through my faults and saw my needs." I had always believed this saying to mean that despite my faults, God blesses me. Now, however, I have a deeper understanding. God considers my faults differently than I do, and certainly differently than the physical world. God knows the origin of my faults; however, God is more concerned with how these flaws can contribute to my development into who God created me to be.

In order for me to arrive at the place of fulfilling my destiny, I need to experience certain circumstances. I need to succeed *and* fail at certain challenges. I need to meet certain people. I need to learn certain lessons. I need to feel certain pains. I need to exuberate with certain joys. I have certain needs according to who I really am—a combination of my creation and my development *(experiences experienced)*. And God understands—sees—all of this, the entire picture from beginning to end. We only see parts at a time, and still those parts are faint glimpses. How can we judge, definitively, with such a limitation?

**Read** 1 Samuel 16:7 *or* Jeremiah 29:10b-14a *or* Psalm 139.

> **Meditate with movement.**
>> **Record your experience(s).**
>>> **Linger in the ending moments.**
>>>> **Carry the ending moments forward into your day.**

## DAY FOUR—*Going to the Source*

Understanding. To understand eternally is a life-long quest. It is something to be sought, consistently, and still it seems that there is so much more to seek.

True understanding of eternal matters can only come from Eternity. That statement seems simple enough. However, many of us seek understanding of such things from other sources that seem authentic, but are not. We prefer these sources, because they give us encouragement and other kinds of good feelings, but these sources do not require much, if anything, from us. Expect from Authenticity a covenant, a requirement from us that is not always easy to fulfill. Actually, most of the time our requirement is not easy to fulfill. How can the finite easily fulfill a requirement from the infinite? Yet also expect the Authentic to be unfailing in fulfilling the other part of the covenant.

When I write about "going to the Source," I do not mean there are times that God is not with us, and we have to find God. Truly, it is more about our tuning in to where God is.

> "We are never without God. But without regular spiritual communion, we forget about our divine nature; we lose the awareness of our spiritual power and ours becomes a halting, feeble existence because we are living without the benefit of our greatest strength."[43]

> ". . . continuous communion with God is the only way to remain conscious of our spiritual nature in the face of our constant daily pressures."[44]

**Read** Matthew 11:28-30 *or* Isaiah 55:6 *or* Luke 11:9-10 *or* Revelation 3:20.
    **Meditate with movement.**
        **Record your experience(s).**
            **Linger in the ending moments.**
                **Carry the ending moments forward into your day.**

## DAY FIVE—Understanding Is Where It's At

*NOTE: This meditation will take you longer than usual to complete.*

Spending time with God is like being exposed to a great light that illuminates all we did not see before this exposure. I believe we have an innate sense of this, even when we may not be consciously aware of this tenet. This innate sense of illumination often keeps us from being in God's presence, because we do not want to see what will be illumined. Remember the warning that we have to get ready to get ready to meditate?

The result of meditation is not only that we realize we are greater than we think. We, also, recognize internal "clutter" that needs to be purged. As human beings, the "stuff" inside is not all divine. It is not all fastened pieces of Eternity. As human beings, some of the stuff inside is quite dirty. It may even be a little "stank." Living from the inside out includes getting a handle on and gaining insight into the parts of ourselves that need to be cleaned up, realigned, repaired—even destroyed.

> "Living from within is an exercise in self-awareness. It requires consistency in exploring the dynamics of your life—being constantly aware of your feelings, attitudes, habits, and motives. As you watch yourself faithfully, you become more aware of what triggers your happy and conflicting emotions, your positive and negative impulses."[45]

Triggers. What a powerful concept. Recovering addicts *(and phobics)* know about them. A trigger is something or someone in our lives which causes us to do something else as a response or reaction. Our responses and reactions to triggers could be positive or negative. However, in this context, I am using the term trigger to refer to responses and reactions that have adverse impacts on our lives.

Often we want to know how to stop destructive behavior or behavior that holds us back. Yet seldom do we really want to know the root causes of the behavior. The roots are where the work is; that is where the not-so-pleasant stuff is.

- What really causes me, a married, mature woman, to flirt with men half my age?
- What really causes me to spank my children for any reason at all?
- What really causes me to draw up in a crowd of more than three people?
- What really causes me to honk my horn loudly and gesture rudely in everyday traffic?
- What really causes me to never raise my hand to disagree with anything?
- What really causes me to write bad checks over and over again?

The roots.

- That is where we will find the boyfriend who broke it off with me in college.
- That is where we will find the abusive father that I never got a chance to confront regarding how much he hurt me.
- That is where we find the rejection.
- That is where we find the workplace in which I am undervalued.
- That is where we find a home where I never get a chance to voice my opinions.
- That is where we find the desire to be loved and accepted at any cost.

Truly, as sure as whatever goes up must come down—whatever goes in has got to come out. In considering the concept of living from the inside out, we tend to only want to consider the good-feeling concept of letting God flow into us so that God's power can flow out of us. Yet we must also consider the other things that get into us that must come out as well. Really, as humans, we are nothing more than vessels.

> "Self-awareness puts you in control of yourself so that you no longer simply react to life, but instead you think critically about what's best for you and consciously decide how you want to be."[46]

- *Understanding* that young men who look like the college boyfriend will cause me to flirt—will aid me in, at least, realizing a potential situation. I still have to *decide* to leave the area where the young man is.
- *Understanding* that I have issues with abuse will aid me in finding professional help and putting distance between myself and my children. I still have to *decide* to make and keep the appointments. I still have to *decide* to count to a number that will allow my anger to cool.
- *Understanding* my past experience(s) with being rejected will aid me in acquiring the confidence to relax and enjoy social gatherings. I still have to *decide* to mingle.
- *Understanding* my need to be valued will aid me in resolving to find other employment. I still have to *decide* to write and hand in my resignation.
- *Understanding* my need to contribute to the vitality of the household will aid me in beginning to believe in the value of my opinions. I still have to *decide* to give them.
- *Understanding* that I try to buy friends is the beginning of better stewardship. I still have to *decide* to leave the checkbook at home.

Recovering addicts understand that once addicted, they live the rest of their lives as an addict. Each day—for some, each moment—is filled with tough decisions to remain healthy. These are decisions that many of us may find easy, even automatic. I contend that all of us, once self-aware, experience the same kind of recovery that an addict does. Our days are filled with opportunities to embrace or to avoid our triggers.

> "Our challenge is to . . . practice living the message . . . listening and talking to God throughout each day," becoming "more conscious of God's indwelling presence, . . . Then we have deeper insight, and a greater understanding of life. Then our duties, cares, and worries become our opportunities for growth, and our burdens are made lighter."[47]

**STUDY** Romans 7:14-25.

Stop afterwards and consider how what Paul is describing fits with your personal struggles, *your* persistent thorn(s) in your flesh.

Then **STUDY** Romans 8:1-17.

Stop afterwards and again, consider how Paul's words minister to your personal struggles, your persistent thorn(s) in your flesh. Now select one (1) verse from what you read in chapter 7 and one (1) verse from what you read in chapter 8. Write them down together with chapter 7's verse coming first and chapter 8's verse following it.

*Read* what you wrote three (3) times.
    **Meditate with movement.**
        **Record your experience(s).**
            **Linger in the ending moments.**
                **Carry the ending moments forward into your day.**

## DAY SIX—*Draw It Out*

So as we live from the inside out, aware of the pleasant and not-so-pleasant parts of ourselves, we realize that we must extract, or draw out that which needs to be purged. Think about a process of drawing out and discarding imperfections, either disease from a human body or flaws from works of art.

These are not easy processes. There is often some resistance to the removal, even if it is for the best. Sometimes the process is quick—sometimes it is not. Actually, oftentimes, the greater the perfection of the desired result—the more rigorous and intense the extraction process is.

While our topic for today is cleansing, we should best understand my use of the image of perfection, especially after our previous discussion regarding God's perspective on our flaws. Perfection is best viewed as complete rather than free of flaws. We should not allow ourselves to enter an ideology that promotes perfection as the absence of defect or blemish. Doing so causes undue and falsely founded condemnation.

Perfection, completion, is—at the end of a creation's existence—a best result of the fulfillment a vision or the implementation of a design, that integrates all that has been refined and all that did not quite get there.

**Read** Isaiah 55:8-13.
> **Meditate with movement.**
>> **Record your experience(s).**
>>> **Linger in the ending moments.**
>>>> **Carry the ending moments forward into your day.**

## DAY SEVEN—What You Habitually Do, You Consistently Are

Let us consider more of the nuggets of truth contained within *In the Spirit*.

In order to live from the inside out, we must make

> ". . . being the guardian of our inner life . . . our highest priority. By ignoring your own spiritual being, you dishonor yourself and risk becoming a pain-filled impostor as you give way to the pressures in your environment."[48]

Remember we have requirements of our Creator.

> ". . . we must be willing to do the work . . . Our inner world is the architect of our external world . . . We aren't happy because we are healthy; we're healthy because we are happy. With our minds we are creating our days; by our choices we are building either the harmony or the pain we experience. The life you are living reflects the life you have already established inside."[49]

> "Living in the spirit isn't complicated. But, it does require continual commitment and devotion."[50]

To be a disciple, a follower of anything, we have to have discipleine—discipline. Successful artists, athletes, business people all regularly contribute excellence to their times of preparation. Then, when they step on the stage, field, or into the boardroom, their performance is unmatched and thusly, greatly rewarded.

Jesus' life, too, was filled with discipline. Just because he was God's only begotten son, he did not have a supernatural connection to his divinity. If he had, that connection would have belied his complete humanity. Rather, habitually, he prayed. Regularly, he attended corporate worship. His spiritual walk was consistent. His spiritual power was consistent as well.

**Read** Mark 1:35, Luke 5:16, *and* Luke 4:16.
> **Meditate with movement.**
>> **Record your experience(s).**
>>> **Linger in the ending moments.**
>>>> **Carry the ending moments forward into your day.**

# *five*

## *free*

*Shortly after joining the church, I became involved quicker than I had planned. Initially, I committed to attending worship two Sundays per month. However, it was not long before I was participating in outreach activities and attending a weekly bible study on how to be led by the Holy Spirit. I began worshipping every Sunday and sometimes, more than one service. Beyond the incredible spiritual growth I was experiencing, I also discovered outstanding fellowship within my church family.*

*I knew where God was again and once again I felt solid in my faith. Furthermore, I developed an intimate relationship with God, learning how to allow the Holy Spirit to guide my life. This knowledge came through practicing meditation. Surely one of the most tangible results of my meditative discipline is the acceptance of my call into professional ministry. Yet the greatest result of this discipline has been what is intangible—my sense of peace and empowerment. Maybe I should write, the return of my sense of peace and empowerment. For it all began at my bedside with Big Mama, continuing under the guidance of the nuns. Somehow, it just got lost . . . buried . . .*

*week four*

## DAY ONE—*Flying*

"What it like to be free, African? What it like?"[51]

Wow. For me, that is the most poignant line in the whole "Roots" miniseries. It arrests me to this day. I would ask, "What it like to be enslaved, Fiddler? What it like?" I cannot imagine what it is like not to come and go as I please. I cannot imagine what it is like not to read and write. I cannot imagine what it is like to have to be aware always of the presence of white people so as to bow and submit myself, publicly, to their perceived sense of superiority in order to stay alive.

That is . . . was my limited understanding of freedom. Is it yours? True freedom is so much more than the ability to not to answer to anyone regarding my schedule, or to be literate, or to be regarded as equal to other ethnicities in the eyes of my government and society.

Several years ago, two of my colleagues challenged me to be free, even to fly. To their challenges, I said not a word, but my crinkled brow and narrowing eyes communicated all of the confusion I felt inside.

*Candi:*
"What do you mean I am not free, that I am not flying?"

*Colleague:*
"Exactly that—you are way too safe."

### And . . .

*Colleague:*
"Has your faith become your god?"

### What did they mean, exactly?

*Candi:*
I take risks, don't I?

*Colleague:*
Nope, not enough.

*Candi:*
But it's not responsible, what you're suggesting. If I did what you're suggesting, I wouldn't be a responsible Christian.

*Colleague:*
What's a responsible Christian?

I do not believe they ever gave me a straight answer—either meandering responses to my inquiries or more questions their tones insisted *I* answer, eventually. And, they were correct in that manner. They were not their answers to provide. Only I had the answers within myself. And, when I thought about it, neither were they the first ones to challenge my . . . responsibility. A few years prior to their onslaught of questions, I had another colleague who challenged me from the way he treated me. I could tell that he understood a part of me, a part that I was bent, bound, and determined to ignore. I was more focused on proving how good I could be. The better I was, the more I believed I could merit favor and blessings from God. How erroneous! I am not blessed because of my goodness. I am blessed, in spite of my feeble attempts at goodness.

My colleagues were in the deep end of the pool enjoying the buoyant support of the water, while I desperately clung to the side of the pool for my righteousness, trying not to drown, when all I had to do was swim. No, all I had to do was float. I was clinging to my good works, to my spiritual disciplines, to my faithful worship attendance, to my 10-12% tithing history, to my practice of celibacy, to my reputation as a sincere Christian. I was quite safe, but I was not enjoying the water. I was not living. Furthermore, what was I doing really to promote the cause of Christ, in a radical way, a way that made a real difference in this world?

**Read** Hebrews 10:35-39.
    **Choose** your method of meditation from one of the prior weeks.

## DAY TWO—Fruit-bearing?

Why did my promotion have to be radical? Because my salvation was. What is more radical than a willing sacrifice for everyone's sins via crucifixion, the most brutal form of capital punishment as an innocent "criminal?" We who believe in Him are called to more than mere discipleship. We are called to radical re-presentation of the One who came to set us captives free.

Free from what, though?

I believe that is the question of this age.

And, the answer is no longer freedom from mere sin. The answer, now, is freedom from what keeps us bound in mere shadows of who we were created to be. We are bound by tradition and outdated doctrine. We fear we will be turned away at the "Pearly Gates" for all sorts of inane reasons, purported by our religious leaders over the millennia, based on all sorts of beliefs, masqueraded as God's will. Let us all stand with fear and trembling, if we ever believe we absolutely know what God's will is! *(My declarations in this book—and in my life—are based on the sentiment of the Merton prayer at the beginning of this book.)*

I was created to exude beauty, intelligence, wit, creativity, compassion, generosity, incredible ability, and passionate sensuality. Who am I—or anyone else—to bridle God's creation?

> "'You need to be very gentle with your spirit . . . It needs to be free, but it also needs you to direct its attention. Too much of one, and not enough of the other, and your spirit will take off like a wild horse . . . If you put it behind a fence, you will kill it. But if you leave it to come and go as it pleases, you will never understand it.'"[52]

If you were to go back to your innermost being, who were you created to be? Are you being her/him every moment of every day? When we deny God's design of ourselves, how do you think God feels about that? What if you lived during Jesus' time on earth and were to encounter him along one of his journeys? Imagine that as he encounters you, he expects to experience you as he created you, but that person is hidden behind layers of superficial and doctrinal holiness . . . well, that is not how I want my script to go. What about you?

**Read** Psalm 139:13-16.
   **Choose** your method of meditation from one of the prior weeks.

## DAY THREE—*Whatever?*

No, I am not advocating reckless abandon and do whatever, however, whenever. Neither am I advocating cheap grace. It is, however, the grace of God from Christ's sacrifice that allows us to be fully human. That is our tension as we seek more of our divinity. Humanity's need for grace to save us from ourselves necessitated Christ's earthly presence, his sacrifice, and his triumph over death. Our belief and confession in him and all that he did for us is all that is required to be saved. Yet the majority of us actually still are trying to live by the Law. We will never make it "in" that way. It is impossible.

So, again, we can just do whatever? Absolutely not. Our relationship with the triune God prevents "whatever." For those of us not in relationship—and we know who we are—we need more of the law to keep us from "whatever." Pursuit of an authentic relationship causes us to be cautious and caring about our thoughts and actions. We do not want to disappoint God. And certainly with freedom comes responsibility—leading to a maturity that is unparalleled with anything any set of laws could produce. I am amazed at what God allows that humans restrict. And what God allows is different for each one of us. That is why a personal relationship is essential. That is why we should not compare ourselves to each other.

> "It is [still about] obedience, not to the Law, but to Grace by faith,
> to the ultimate absurdity of a God who gives Jerusalem for free."[53]

Here is where I greatly experience God as a parent. We were not created to be children forever. God teaches and nurtures us with the expectation that one day we will be mature adults. As a parent, I get this concept. When my daughter is grown, I do not expect her to continue to ask me how to wash clothes, or what is the best way to cook rice, or whether she ought to date someone with a questionable reputation? So, why should I still ask God similar questions regarding my life and my spirituality? By now, I ought to be able to discern situations and make good decisions at a rather advanced level. Exercise of this ability allows me to grow even further and for God to permit/present to me greater and greater depths of this life. Wherever we are in God—beginner, intermediate, advanced, etc.—we ought to be striving for the next level instead of being content—and safe—at a place that we believe we have conquered.

**Read** Romans 14:1-12.
**Choose** your method of meditation from one of the prior weeks.

## *DAY FOUR—Bodied*

Total freedom also includes an appreciation, an embrace, and a love for our bodies. They are extraordinary and beautiful. When and where, exactly, did the flawed notion begin that our bodies are inherently evil? And as a Christian, I cannot recall one Sunday school lesson that taught me to love it and take care of it. Do you? Why are we considered most holy when we suppress them and their energies? How can we be whole when we fear and even imprison a powerful part of our selves? I simply do not believe that God intended for us to regard our bodies this way.

> "The beginning of the true teaching is that God made man—and precisely what we ordinarily mean by man: eyes, ears, nose, arms, buttocks, shinbones, ankles, toenails—God made all that, not just a 'soul' in his image. And the end of the true teaching is that God redeemed man—flesh, bones, and all things appertaining to the perfection of human nature, by the Resurrection of the Body of Jesus."[54]

I had been long suspicious, but I earnestly began to question the Church's fear of our bodies when I began to dance in worship services. To even allow dance in the sanctuary had been a long-fought battle with Church leadership. When the battle was finally won, we dancers had to move gracefully through our three layers of tight clothing and race to the restrooms after ministering to wipe the sheets of sweat from our limited exposed areas. Shortly after I began dancing, I attended a performance of the Alvin Ailey dancers, seeing them anew. I had witnessed their majesty before, but this time, I was totally enraptured by their beauty. This time I was completely affected by the length of their limbs, the cuts in their muscles and how their muscles relaxed and contracted with every movement, how the parts of the body integrated to create such stunning art. All of this is lost in worship, the best place for it, because of fear—no, because of a phobia—regarding our bodies.

What it like to be free, Church? What it like?

Does anyone else see/sense how most of our religious organizations today are more like the Pharisees and Sadducees than we are like Jesus? It is a bit scary for me when I think about it. If Jesus returned for his church today, what would he find indeed? What would he do? Spew us out of his mouth as lukewarm? Probably.

**Read** Galatians 5:1,13 and 2:19-20.

**Choose** your method of meditation from one of the prior weeks.

## DAY FIVE—*From Here to Eternity*

Are you really ready to experience all of life, every bit of it? Are you really ready to live into your eternity? If so, keep going. If not, take some time to ponder and come back when you are ready.

_____

Now that you're ready, read the following passages from the 8th chapter of Romans, The Living Bible:

> "If God is for us, who can ever be against us? Since God did not spare even his own Son, but gave him up for us all, won't God, who gave us Christ, also give us everything else?
>
> "Who dares accuse us whom God has chosen for his own? Will God? No! He is the one who has given us right standing with himself. Who then will condemn us? Will Christ Jesus? No, for he is the one who died for us, . . .
>
> "Can anything ever separate us from Christ's love? . . . No, . . .
>
> ". . . I am convinced that nothing can ever separate us from his love. Death can't, and life can't. The angels can't, and the demons can't. Our fears for today, our worries about tomorrow, and even the powers of hell can't keep God's love away. Whether we are high above the sky or in the deepest ocean, nothing in all creation will ever be able to separate us from the love of God that is revealed in Christ Jesus our Lord."[55]

**Read** Romans 8:37 from a traditional version of the Bible *(King James, New International, etc.)* three (3) times. Chew on it. What does it mean to you, specifically? With your answer(s) in mind:

**Choose** your method of meditation from one of the prior weeks.

## DAY SIX—*New-Bigger-Greater*

Jesus tells us in the 14th chapter of John that we will do greater works than He did while He was on earth, because He is now in Heaven and has sent the Holy Spirit to us.

Too often we believe God only for the smaller things. Let's stop that. Let's even stop limiting God to what God has done before now. During a televised episode of "Praise the Lord" on the Trinity Broadcasting Network, in October 2002, Bishop T.D. Jakes exhorted us to recognize that what God has done for others is great. However, God is waiting to do for us what has never been done before. No matter what miracles we have witnessed or heard about—God has more in store for God's people—if we just go beyond the familiar.

Familiar is old news. Once the testimony, no matter how powerful, is shared—it is old news. It is wonderful for history and for encouragement, but that was yesterday. What is today's headline?

**Read** John 14:12 three (3) times.

**Choose** your method of meditation from one of the prior weeks.

## DAY SEVEN—*Forever Free*

Perhaps you resist the greater works because of not wanting your ego to inflate. You do not want to get "the big head." However, if you walk with God, if you are walking with Eternity—that will not happen. I promise; you will remain humble. God will see to that.

Additionally, if you refrain from the greater works because of your wanting to avoid inflating your ego, that is not humility. That is cowardice. That is fear—either of the ego itself, of making mistakes, or of *how* God will keep you humble.

Instead, remember who you are. You are the one with Eternity fastened to your soul. You can make good—even excellent choices. You know that you are saved. You know how to meditate, to pray, to seek God's face. You know how to call down heaven. You know how to repent and get back up again when you fall. What else do you need, little God-one? Put your foot out there and go for the greater. Ask God for things that get God excited. Ask for the things that stir God up.

Go for it and I'll see you in eternity—eternity on earth.

**Read** Joshua 1:9 three (3) times.

**Choose** your method of meditation from one of the prior weeks.

## six

### be

*Without my personal relationship with God I would not know who I am. Today, I find that to be the greatest benefit of meditation. To know who I am is so incredibly invaluable to my quality of life. I am about twice the age of that young, lost, and empty—no drying out—girl sitting at the edge of the oasis in Gainesville, Florida. Certainly, I know way more than I did then. However, I am still discovering who I am. Maybe self-discovery is inextricably linked to God-discovery. How much do we limit ourselves because of our limited first-hand knowledge of God? As I have allowed myself over the last few years to experience God in unconventional ways, the boundaries of my selfhood have expanded. And you know what, I look forward to those boundaries, eventually, disappearing altogether. My God has no boundaries. Why should I?*

I preached, once likening true worship of God as simply be-ing. The text was John 4:4-24. And, the title was "Just Worship." At the end I extolled the congregation—just be.

Below is an updated excerpt from that sermon:

---

Since the beginning of time, humans have always known of an entity—a force at least—that is greater than ourselves. We have spent an eternity trying to describe it . . . him . . . her—trying to get our heads around, trying to understand, even trying to control this being that we cannot see, but that we experience every moment of every day of our lives. Our behavior with and toward this entity runs the gamut. We deny this supreme power when we become frustrated with its existence, or its participation or seeming non-participation in our lives. We betray this creator/sustainer when we think someone or something else might help us attain a goal a little easier or a little faster. And somewhere in the midst of all of this interaction we worship this being. Humanity has an innate desire to worship someone or something. We have to praise, we have to lift up a person, an object, a concept. Well, we as Christians direct this innate desire to worship towards a being we call God, Yahweh, Jesus, Holy Spirit.

But what is worship really? What does it mean to worship God? Why is it necessary? What does it look like? How does it feel? When do we do it? Is there one, right way to worship?

Let us quest for answers to these questions with the account of a woman who went to draw water at a historic well around noontime where she met a man, a stranger, who changed her life forever. This life-changing tale is recorded in the Gospel of John 4th chapter, 4th-24th verses.

So, the narrative commences with a meeting between the human and the divine, between the finite and the infinite, between the temporal and the eternal. Jesus is making his way to Galilee via Samaria and decides to stop for a moment to rest at a well. A Samaritan woman is making her way to this same well to draw water. Their destinies intersect at this certain time in history. It is one of these special times, when if one of them had delayed their journey by one minute or two, they may have missed each other. But, they didn't. They are right on course, to encounter each other in this space, just at this time.

The Gospel writer does not give her a name, but for our purposes, let's call her Diamond. Diamond is the sister-girl whom we all know—making her life work with what she's got—intelligence, beauty, wit, ingenuity, determination—qualities necessary to maneuver through an uneven playing field riddled with the results of racial, sexual, class, social, and religious discrimination. She's got personality, a sense of style, charisma, resilience, and an interesting blend of self-confidence and challenged self-esteem. She rises from her bed each day, dreading what she dreads, and hoping what she hopes. She cares for herself and those she cares about. She provides for those without provision, wondering if there will ever be someone to provide for her. And, while Diamond prays the prayers of her ancestors to a being greater than herself whom she calls YHWH *(Yahweh)*, somewhere deep inside herself, in her spirit, in her gut, in her knower—she suspects that something is missing. Something is not fulfilled, but she doesn't know where exactly to get it. She's tried filling it with work—still empty. She's tried filling it with friends—still empty. She's tried filling it with serving the poor—still empty. She's tried filling it with varied male companionship—eventually, still empty.

After awhile, Diamond convinces herself that she's either been paranoid or she's become gullible enough to believe that this great sense of peace and joy and abundant life, that crosses her lips each time she prays the scriptures, is for her too. Eventually, she understands they are mere words on paper, bound in a book given to her at her baptism, just concepts to ponder, just traditions to uphold. They will never manifest into anything meaningfully substantive in her life. So, rather than continue to live in constant disappointment with these unmet expectations of filling her void, she stops her search. She ceases seeking. She discontinues knocking. Diamond is persuaded that she will find nothing, and no one will open the door.

Then, there comes this day, a day that started out as any other day—full of routine, including a visit to the well for water. "Would you give me a drink of water," comes the voice of the male stranger.

"Would you give me a drink of water," Jesus asked Diamond.

And, how does Diamond respond? With questions—lots of them and plenty points of contention. "How come You, a Jewish man, are asking me, a Samaritan woman, for a drink of water?" When God asks us to serve God, what is our answer? "How come You, God, are asking me, an incapable, mistaken-ridden human to do . . . this?" And, God's response is to us as it was then, "If you only understood what I had to offer, You would be asking me for what I asked you."

Worship is our time with God to love on each other—like any sincerely fulfilling relationship. Ya just be in each other's presence just 'cause ya wanna be there. You like each other's essence, touch, smell, laugh, jokes, insight, even the differences between you, because it's the differences which challenge you to become a better you.

Howard Thurman writes,

> "The central fact in religious experience is the awareness of meeting God. The descriptive words used are varied: sometimes it is called an encounter; sometimes a confrontation; and sometimes, a sense of Presence . . . {S}he is face to face with something which is so much more—and so much more inclusive—than all of {her} awareness of {her}self that for her, *in the moment*, there are no questions. Without asking, somehow {s}he knows."[56]

Well, it's obvious that while Diamond is full of doubt and debate she has not yet entered into a place of worship, though she is in the very presence of Jesus—face to face. We all know what it's like to be right next to somebody and yet not be engaged with them. All we see are the barriers between us—when there is something far greater that connects us—if we would simply allow ourselves to just be. Diamond has not entered worship yet; she is talking a bit too much—in this context, asking too many questions—continuing to debate the ancient question of the appropriate place to worship—continuing to try to make this infinite God to be one kind of deity or the other—the God of the Jews or the God of the Samaritans, when in fact God was God of both peoples, and if she takes the time to just be . . . to just be in Jesus' presence, to just be in the moment, there would have been no questions. Without asking, somehow she would have known.

But again—Diamond had stopped hoping, ceased believing and had allowed herself to lose her passion for life. She had become caught up in her routine, where there is no room for the Divine to simply show up in her life and just be.

The good news is that God is so wonderfully patient, as Jesus demonstrates by continuing to answer Diamond's questions in ways that entice her to come closer, deeper into his Presence.

"If you, Diamond, drink the water I have to give you, instead of all the other beverages you've sought to quench your desires, you will never be thirsty again—ever."

Sensing an opening, Jesus moves a little closer, creatively eliciting a confession about her life that Diamond probably doesn't normally discuss with a stranger. Jesus moves to a private place with precision and accuracy.

Thurman writes,

> "What is insisted upon, however, without regard to the term used, is that in the experience defined as religious, the individual is seen as being exposed to direct knowledge of ultimate meaning, *ne plus ultra* being, in which all that the individual is, becomes clear as immediate and often distinct revelation."[57]

ALL of who Diamond is in this very moment becomes clear, with immediate and distinct revelation. In worship, we not only learn who God is, we learn who we are.

Even in this revelatory moment, though, Diamond's not quite at worship yet. She is almost there, but she pulls back. He is a little too close. He knows a little too much. So she challenges his knowledge, sarcastically, calls him a prophet, and tests him on the difference between where his and her folk worship.

Patience responds, "Believe me, Diamond, the time will come when your folk will worship God neither here nor where my folk worship. The time will come, well actually, it has already come when what you are called and where you go for a worship service will not matter."

Patience continues to explain, "What matters is who you are and how you live your life. These are the kinds of worshippers the Lord seeks. Simple, honest, and true—just like God—a pure Spirit. God is a Spirit and those who decide to worship God must do so in Spirit and in Truth."

Hmmm . . . something about what he is saying resonates in her spirit, but she can't quite get her head around it. She can't quite let go and receive this concept of Spirit and Truth. To do that takes the ability to expect, the ability to hope for the peace, joy, and abundance she prayed for just that morning. But, remember she'd given up on those short-term blessings and given in to routine. Yet somewhere deep inside there remains a hope for a longer term blessing. It is this place deep inside that Patience persists in reaching. Longer term blessings are easier to hold onto than shorter term ones, because when they don't come, they're not missed because they're far off. So, there is no risk in Diamond's hope for a Messiah whom she would probably not meet in her lifetime. She tells the Stranger, "I don't know about all this you're telling me, but I do know that when the Messiah comes, I'll get the whole story."

That's when the revelation hit—"I am the One you seek. I am your Messiah." All Jesus needs is a little entry of hope, even one rooted in longer term expectations. "I am the One you seek. I am your Messiah."—right here, right now. I am your Deliverance today, not when you get to heaven. I am your Provision in this very moment, not when you get your promotion. I am your Healing right now, not after your surgery. Believe me now, worship me now, now—today. Let go and worship me—right here, right now.

In this very moment, Diamond enters his Presence and worships. After this moment of revelation I believe part of the story doesn't make the manuscript. Maybe the writer simply didn't have the words to describe what happened. After the revelation, I believe there is a time of ecstasy—Diamond makes it into the holy of holies, into the throne room, into the inner chamber. She is where deep calls unto deep and there are no more questions. She simply somehow knows and she stays there, basking in the glory of her Creator. And, Jesus stays there with her too, basking in the glory of his creation.

That's why she leaves her water jar. That's why Jesus doesn't want the food the disciples, caught up in their routine, insist that he eat. Deep is calling unto and responding to deep. There is no room for water jars and food.

Suddenly, Diamond can conquer the world. She overflows with peace, joy, and abundance—so much so that she can't keep it to herself. She flees back to town with a compelling unction to tell somebody—anybody. "Come. Come with me. Come meet a man who looked at me and saw straight through to the depths of my soul."

The invitation is the same today—come, gather, meet God, be in God's Presence, know who God is and more fully who you are. Just come and be. Just worship. Just be.

# *afterthought*

If he had been . . .

But he wouldn't have been for me
Because he couldn't even be for himself
So now when I grieve him
I grieve that—
That I didn't understand him . . . understand us
Better
I grieve that he didn't find a way here, where I am
For himself

I can't blame him now
Nor the ones he could've blamed
They've all passed on

But I'm not
I'm alive
I can choose not to abandon those I love
Even when loving them causes me pain from time to time
I can choose not to sacrifice myself for those I love
Even when loving me causes them pain from time to time

I am strong and wise and triumphant
My scar tissue enables me to land and take off again

I am free to be me
Fully free and fully me

This is who I was meant to be
Full and free
And my fullness
May make you nervous
But he IS here to defend me
By my knowing I'm not me alone
He was me before me
'Cause I'm more like him than anybody else
Only he can help me be
The me that I am
But only me can protect me
He didn't have to know how to be a father to me
God knew—knew us both
God always knew
So, now yes, he knows too
And I'm taking him with me—in the air
As I fly
Fully free . . .
And fully me.

# *notes*

1   Thomas Merton, *Thoughts in Solitude* (The Abbey of Our Lady of Gethsemani, 1956), 16.

2   Howard Thurman, *The Inward Journey* (Friends United Press: Richmond, Indiana, 1961), 90.

3   Karol K. Truman, *Feelings Buried Alive Never Die . . .* (Olympus Distributing: Las Vegas, 1991), 3.

4   Ibid, 5.

5   Ibid, 161-162.

6   Ibid, 164-165.

7   Ibid, 70-71.

8   Merriam-Webster, Inc., *Merriam-Webster's Desk Dictionary* (Springfield, Massachusetts, 1995).

9   Charlotte Parnell, *Meditation: A Beginner's Guide* (Barnes and Noble Books: New York, 2001), 24.

10  Jon Kabat-Zinn, *Wherever You Go There You Are: Mindfulness Meditation in Everyday Life* (Hyperion: New York, 1994), xvii.

11  Kabat-Zinn, xviii.

12  Ibid, 4.

13  Ann Landers.

14  Kabat-Zinn, 27.

15  Mike Murdock, *The Leadership Secrets of Jesus* (Honor Books: Tulsa, Oklahoma, 1996), 13.

16  Ecclesiastes 1:2c

17  Ecclesiastes 1:14

18  Parnell, 28.

19  Karasmatic Consulting, "Relax and Rest", 2002.

20  Merriam-Webster.

21  Kenneth E. Bruscia, *Defining Music Therapy* (Barcelona Publishers, Gilsum: New Hampshire, 1998), 104.

22  Hal A. Lingerman, *The Healing Energies of Music* (The Theosophical Publishing

House, Wheaton, Illinois, 1983), 3.
[23] Lingerman, 2-3.
[24] Lingerman, 34.
[25] Kabat-Zinn, 8.
[26] Ibid.
[27] Ibid.
[28] Ibid.
[29] Kabat-Zinn, 31.
[30] Ibid.
[31] Ibid, 31-32.
[32] Quotable Magnets. Author unknown.
[33] Mark 4:38 (The Living Bible).
[34] Kabat-Zinn, 87.
[35] Murdock, 30.
[36] Kabat-Zinn., 87-88.
[37] John 4:14b
[38] Upper Room Ministries, "Life's Borders," (General Board of Discipleship: Nashville, August 28, 2002).
[39] Ibid.
[40] Ibid.
[41] Howard Thurman, *The Creative Encounter* (Friends United Press: Richmond, Indiana, 1954), 26.
[42] Ibid, 27.
[43] Susan L. Taylor, *In the Spirit* (Amistad: New York, 1993), 3.
[44] Ibid, 4.
[45] Ibid.
[46] Ibid, 5.
[47] Ibid.
[48] Ibid, 2.
[49] Ibid, 3.
[50] Ibid, 4.
[51] *Roots: The Miniseries*, made-for-television, 8 episodes, (American Broadcasting Company, 1977).
[52] Michael E. Gerber, *The EMyth Revisited: Why Most Small Business Don't Work and What to Do About It* (HarperBusiness: New York, 1995), 158.
[53] Robert Farrar Capon, *Hunting the Divine Fox: Images and Mystery in Christian Faith* (The Seabury Press: New York, 1974), 54.
[54] Ibid, 80.
[55] Romans 8:31-39, The Living Bible.
[56] Thurman, 23-24.
[57] Ibid, 24.

# bibliography

Bruscia, Kenneth E. *Defining Music Therapy*. Barcelona Publishers, Gilsum: New Hampshire. 1998.

Capon, Robert Farrar. *Hunting the Divine Fox: Images and Mystery in Christian Faith*. The Seabury Press: New York. 1974.

Gerber, Michael E. *The EMyth Revisited: Why Most Small Business Don't Work and What to Do About It*. HarperBusiness: New York. 1995.

Haley, Alex. "Roots: The Miniseries." American Broadcasting Company. 1977.

Kabat-Zinn, Jon. *Wherever You Go There You Are: Mindfulness Meditation in Everyday Life*. Hyperion: New York. 1994.

Karasmatic Consulting. 2002.

Landers, Ann.

Lingerman, Hal A. *The Healing Energies of Music*. The Theosophical Publishing House, Wheaton, Illinois. 1983.

Merriam-Webster, Inc. *Merriam-Webster's Desk Dictionary*. Springfield, Massachusetts. 1995.

Merton, Thomas. *Thoughts in Solitude*. The Abbey of Our Lady of Gethsemani. 1956.

Murdock, Mike. *The Leadership Secrets of Jesus*. Honor Books: Tulsa, Oklahoma. 1996.

Parnell, Charlotte. *Meditation: A Beginner's Guide*. Barnes and Noble Books: New York. 2001.

Quotable Magnets.

Taylor, Susan L. *In the Spirit*. Amistad: New York. 1993.

Thurman, Howard. *The Creative Encounter*. Friends United Press: Richmond, Indiana. 1954.

_____. *The Inward Journey*. Friends United Press: Richmond, Indiana. 1961.

Truman, Karol K. *Feelings Buried Alive Never Die* . . . Olympus Distributing: Las Vegas. 1991.

Upper Room Ministries. General Board of Discipleship: Nashville. 2002.